BEYOND AND ALONE!

---

*The Theme of Isolation in Selected Short Fiction
of Kate Chopin, Katherine Anne Porter,
and Eudora Welty*

Hiroko Arima

University Press of America,® Inc.
Lanham · Boulder · New York · Toronto · Oxford

Copyright © 2006 by
University Press of America,® Inc.
4501 Forbes Boulevard
Suite 200
Lanham, Maryland 20706
UPA Acquisitions Department (301) 459-3366

PO Box 317
Oxford
OX2 9RU, UK

Library of Congress Control Number: 2006923338
ISBN-13: 978-0-7618-3480-9 (paperback : alk. paper)
ISBN-10: 0-7618-3480-X (paperback : alk. paper)

Dedicated to deceased S. A.

To F. A., Y. A., and M. A.

Table of Contents

Preface

"Place and writer sustain each other" (viii), Jan Nordby Gretlund, a noted Welty scholar, states in the preface to *Eudora Welty's Aesthetics of Place*. Gretlund's book explores the depth of the impact of place in Welty's fiction and its aesthetic influence upon her art. It is well known that Welty was born, grew up, and stayed in Jackson, Mississippi. In a somewhat similar manner, Kate Chopin's and Katherine Anne Porter's fiction are subtly or directly rooted in particular places—Louisiana and St. Louis, Missouri, for Chopin, and Texas for Porter. The relationships between these particular places in the South and the three authors are, of course, as different as their individual personalities are different. Throughout the long period during which I worked on the manuscript of this book, in the very beginning as a graduate student who was about to launch on the long (in my case) project of a dissertation, the varying and interweaving hues and textures that the connections between places and the three authors and their works exuded continued to sustain me. The uniqueness of each of their characters and their works is so striking that it almost seemed to completely defy any scholarly attempt to discuss them together. Yet similarities and common aspects of their personalities, their works, and places with which each of them is firmly related continued to loom before me in ways that totally evade such dichotomous polarities as alikeness and unlikeness. Consequently I ended up quite captivated in the attempt to combine the examination of the works of these three authors, while being drawn to each particular one of them at times because of the strong character of each. Whereas it has been logically entirely justifiable to analyze them in the same manuscript, as I explain in the first chapter, what came out of the task of examining their works side by side matched the fascination of weaving or painting where one seeks and experiments with the merging and conflicting patterns and shades. Talking about one example of complexities that such shades present, James T. F. Tanner aptly points to the troubled relationship between Porter and Texas, while examining her tie to it in *The Texas Legacy of Katherine Anne Porter* (Tanner 2). Kate Chopin was a "bilingual and bicultural" person, living in both English-speaking and French-speaking cultures in St.

Louis, New Orleans, and northwestern Louisiana (Koloski xi). The differences between the experiences in their lives in terms of their relationships to places were a subject that sustained my interest for years, although such biographical facts are not the central theme of this book.

Kate Chopin, Katherine Anne Porter and Eudora Welty were also different in their life experiences, including their marital status. However, I revere these authors too much to even mention the facts of their lives specifically, although, as facts, such matters concerning them are known among scholars, students and readers. The point I would like to bring up by the brief reference to such facts is the authors' extremely individualistic and private natures, which I also revere tremendously and which also have been the second important source of the inspiration for me for this project; although, again, this book in itself does not directly deal with biographical factors, either. What is pointed out as their very "private" natures by scholars who summed up biographical information about them has always been another, and perhaps, the strongest fascination for me. Welty is famous for her intensely "private" nature. This is reflected in her famous essay, "Must the Novelist Crusade?" which I discuss at length in the beginning of Chapter 4, an essay which underpins the philosophical foundation of this research. The subtlety and sensitivity of the ideas and the philosophy that Welty presented in this essay not only justify the theme of this book, isolation, but also envelop it. My greatest debt is to Welty's essay. Precisely because Welty was an intensely private person, she was also intensely sensitive about others' inner selves. In describing the extent of her private nature, the term, intense, seems the most appropriate. Despite its depth, the phrase, "fiercely private," would not have applied to Welty. The phrase better describes Porter's character. Porter's fierceness in her pursuit of ideals and places where she could fit in is also reflected in the characters that she created, the most significant of whom is Miranda in "Old Mortality," treated at the end of Chapter 4 and used to conclude this book in the last chapter. "Old Mortality" is another philosophical foundation of this research and the great debt in respect to the theme of isolation. Scholars have referred to Porter's struggles with various relationships and her aloofness and isolation. One example, mentioned above, is her "uneasy" relationship with the Texas where she was born; another example is what Joan Givner mentions as her "hysteria" over being alone (Givner 317). On the surface her defiance and fear are differing and opposing aspects of her life, but they are both the results of her private self and private pursuit. Lorraine Nye Eliot states that Chopin was a "very private person" and that her family and friends "respected her privacy" (Eliot x). The concepts of privacy and isolation may not be entirely synonymous, but it cannot be denied that such private natures of the three authors have continued to attract many scholars to the study of biographical connections in the works of Chopin, Porter, and Welty. This is true with this book, too.

The third debt of this research is to a particular town in Texas—Denton. On a personal note, this debt is actually the most significant in terms of practical struggles towards the completion of this project. As may be noted, Denton,

Texas, is a city located to the northeast of Dallas, where three cities, Dallas, Fort Worth and Denton form a triangle, and is the home of the University of North Texas, exactly where this project began. On the northern side of Denton runs Loop 288. If one drives towards the east on this road, one travels towards the deeper south, which in short means that the vegetation will be deeper and greener, and scenes more swampy. If one drives towards the west, the vegetation will be less, and scenes more rocky and brown. Denton is situated in the middle of two such kinds of landscapes, and there the vegetation is quite green, but not very profuse, and there are hardly any tall trees. The land is vast. The summer of course is intensely hot, but the air is very dry. Except during the short winter, throughout the year there are days of very high temperature, not only in the middle of the summer. When it rains there, it pours, as a saying goes, often becoming thunder storms. I would describe the climate and the geography there as flat, vast, green, and intense. Because of the expanse of the land and the dry air, the sunset that could be seen on the edge of the university area was indescribable. Wild Blue Bonnets are the Texas state flower. Along with Blue Bonnets, red Indian paint brush and pale-pink prairie roses bloom in May. The climate, geography, and nature of Denton sustained me through my years as a graduate student there and throughout this project. It has been precisely because of my attachment to the nature in Denton that I pursued my degree there and persisted with this project, and this is why Gretlund's phrase above became so real: "Place and writer sustain each other." So far I have not had an opportunity to visit Chopin's St. Louis and Louisiana, places in Texas where Porter was, or Welty's Jackson, Mississippi, but because of the way I was so drawn to the climate and the landscape of Denton, this phrase is genuine to me—not exactly for my personal experiences, but rather because the place, Denton, enhanced my understanding of the relationships between particular places in the south and the three writers. The southern landscape in which I fortunately lived, for a time, is very different from what the three authors were related to, but I would like to be permitted to say today that the attachment to the climate and geography of a particular place in the south is something I share with all three of them. I dedicate this book to the nature in Denton, particularly because in so many spots in Denton such nature has been destroyed by rapid development in the past decade. Therefore, although I describe the nature there, it is with the sense of a great loss that so much of it exists now only in memory. To tell the truth, most of the personal relationships that were formed during the years of my study there have faded away, but the relationship between the place and this project has persisted despite the destruction of the nature there.

On a scholarly side I owe this book to Dr. James T. F. Tanner, a professor at the University of North Texas, and Dr. J. F. K. Kobler, a former professor there. I wrote the manuscript of this book under the supervision of Dr. Tanner, the author of *The Texas Legacy of Katherine Anne Porter,* who suggested that I write a study of these three authors whose works I was already familiar with through classes at the graduate school of the English Department of the University of North Texas. At the completion of this book, I would like to express gratitude to Dr. Tanner again. I also would like to express my gratitude to Dr. Kobler, particularly for the course he offered in the summer of 1993, titled "Modernist Fiction," in which he introduced us to the short fiction of Katherine Mansfield, Ernest Hemingway, James Joyce, and Anton Chekhov. Despite the great number of courses I took as a student at universities and graduate schools both in Japan and the U.S.A., this course is now most relevant to this book, and even more importantly relevant to the direction of my future research based on this book. That is, looking back, starting from the exposure to the significance of the genre, short fiction, in Dr. Kobler's course, and through writing this manuscript as a dissertation, and finally through the process of completing this book, the possibility of further study in short fiction has occurred to me. Above all, during the past year when I was revising and adding to the manuscript, the possibility of studying Eudora Welty's fiction along with that of Chekhov started to grow in my mind. Thus Dr. Kobler's course is a significant point on the same long time line that shows the writing of this book and the future research I envision.

Here I would like to add another mention of place. Last year, I traveled to Moscow. Since I was then already familiar with the works by Chekhov through Dr. Kobler's course and through my study of Welty, this trip considerably increased my interest in the Russian writer. Jan Nordby Gretlund, Marion Montgomery, and other Welty scholars have discussed the relationship between Welty and Chekhov. Needless to say, Welty's famous essay, "Reality in Chekhov's Stories" has inspired scholars to compare Welty and Chekhov. Gretlund devotes his last chapter to the discussion of the comparison between Welty and Chekhov. He writes; "people feel isolated everywhere, be it in the Russian town of S---, San Francisco, Morgana, or Jackson. Living in a family is no guarantee against loneliness" (336). Human struggle and strife apart, it is blissful that in Moscow, and other cities and towns in Russia, traditional culture and nature are today still intact. The preserved quality of Russian places evoked in me a strong interest in the studies by American scholars who have traced the connections between American and Russian writers. Montgomery, for example, discusses similarities and dissimilarities between Welty and Faulkner, and among Chekhov, Dostoevsky and Tolstoï (4-7, 19-20, 178-79). Especially pertinent to my work is Lorraine Nye Eliot's new biographical approach to Chopin's works, published in the second year of this new century and based on close textual reading, in which she points to the influence of Chekhov on Chopin's *The Awakening* (Eliot 113-14).

I would like to express my gratitude to the staff of University Press of America and Joanne Foeller of Timely Publication Services for their understanding and patience. I owe them thanks for the publication of this book and the practical assistance for this project.

December, 2005
Tokyo, Japan
Hiroko Arima

Acknowledgments

I acknowledge with gratitude the right to reproduce material from several sources. For works by Kate Chopin: Reprinted by permission of Louisiana State University Press from *The Complete Works of Kate Chopin*, edited by Per Seyersted, copyright © 1969, 1997 by Louisiana State University Press.

For works by Katherine Anne Porter: Excerpts from "María Concepción," "He," "The Jilting of Granny Weatherall" and "Flowering Judas" from *Flowering Judas and Other Stories*, copyright © 1930 and renewed 1958 by Katherine Anne Porter, reprinted by permission of Harcourt, Inc. Excerpts from "The Old Order" copyright © 1936 and renewed 1964 by Katherine Anne Porter, reprinted by permission of Harcourt, Inc. Excerpt from "Old Mortality" in *Pale Horse, Pale Rider: Three Short Novels*, copyright © 1937 and renewed 1965 by Katherine Anne Porter, reprinted by permission of Harcourt, Inc.

For works by Eudora Welty: Excerpts from "A Memory" and "Flowers for Marjorie" in *A Curtain of Green and Other Stories*, copyright © 1937 and renewed 1965 by Eudora Welty, reprinted by permission of Harcourt, Inc. Excerpts from "The Whistle" and "A Curtain of Green" in *A Curtain of Green and Other Stories*, copyright © 1938 and renewed 1966 by Eudora Welty, reprinted by permission of Harcourt, Inc. Excerpts from "Death of a Traveling Salesman" in *A Curtain of Green and Other Stories*, copyright © 1941 and renewed 1969 by Eudora Welty, reprinted by permission of Harcourt, Inc. Excerpts from "At the Landing" in *The Wide Net and Other Stories*, copyright © 1943 and renewed 1971 by Eudora Welty, reprinted by permission of Harcourt, Inc.

For the poem of Emily Dickinson used to conclude this book in the last chapter: Reprinted by permission of the publishers and the Trustees of Amherst College from *The Poems of Emily Dickinson*, Ralph W. Franklin, ed., Cambridge, Mass.: The Belknap Press of Harvard University Press, copyright © 1998 by the President and Fellows of Harvard College, copyright © 1951, 1955, 1979, 1983 by the President and Fellows of Harvard College.

Chapter 1

Writers, Isolation, and Selected Short Fiction of Kate Chopin, Katherine Anne Porter, and Eudora Welty

The task of writing demands privacy and loneliness from the writer. So does the task of reading. Some artists are willing to obey the severity of the call from the art of creation, its demand to keep oneself solitary while in the act of creating. Others obey this command hesitantly. For instance, Katherine Anne Porter went through both willingness and reluctance to obey the order of artistic creation that strongly required her to be alone. In her existed both headstrong will and determination to create and vulnerability and fear of being by herself. At one time, she mentioned that the toil and requirement of writing were not compatible with human comradeship and domestic life. But, as Joan Givner observes, there was also a time when she was actually "filled . . . with horror" by "the thought of living alone for the rest of her life" and "reacted almost with hysteria to the attention" from another individual (317).

As in living, the task in reading, writing, and in creative art is the task of facing solitude. It amazes, and sometimes appalls, some individuals when they face the abyss of aloneness in the midst of passionate embraces. It quite terrifies them when they suddenly peer into the immeasurable depth of the darkness of solitariness, the bottom of which they can never see, just when they feel that finally they had entered the merciful end of their long isolation in the romantic fusion with another individual. Both Elaine Showalter and Margaret Culley aptly quote De Maupassant's "Solitude," pointing to the significant fact that Chopin translated this story for a St. Louis magazine.[1] They both emphasize that it was compatible with the core of Chopin's thought about the existential solitary state of each human being. Showalter mentions in the article that the words in the story from De Maupassant were tangible for Kate Chopin. Chopin had grown to realize "the existential solitude of all human beings" after having overcome the illusion of lifelong ties with others in various forms of companionship such as "friendship, romance, marriage, or even motherhood" (Showalter 33). Lorraine Nye Eliot also observes what she describes as Chopin's "very private" nature in her recently published new biography of Chopin, *The Real Kate Chopin*, closely discussing the common preoccupation of Chopin and Maupassant with dark themes such as "night" and "solitude" (x, 99).

In reading through short fiction by Katherine Anne Porter, Eudora Welty, and Kate Chopin, one observes that the theme of fundamental isolation permeates many of them. "The existential solitude" of all human beings underlies various forms of isolation that we see in their short fiction. Although the nature of isolation of characters in each story examined in this book varies depending on situational and social circumstances, and on their sex, age, and class, the undercurrent of all of their lone struggles is the existential isolation of all humans. Any form of seeming togetherness cannot wipe it out. Just as not a few artists cringe when confronting the artistic requirement of keeping to themselves, many individuals suffer, crave and try to crawl out of the pit of solitude.

Kate Chopin, however, was aware that satisfying one's need to have relationships with others and to belong can conflict with one's need to establish one's autonomy and sovereignty and that merely fleeing from isolation does not entirely satisfy one. A person has both drives, to be oneself and to be together with others (Skaggs 1). Chopin knew that these two needs go together to form an individual's identity, although they might not be compatible (Skaggs 1). In observing human nature and in examining the works of art that successfully grasp the complexity of human psychology and behavior, we cannot completely separate these two poles. Rather, the two opposing poles always merge into each other, and then break and divide again the next moment, always changing the patterns of a character's psychology and the nature of isolation. At times a character struggles to escape from the darkness of isolation. Then at another time, the same individual may desire to shut away the intrusion of others and may prefer to rest in the mercy, quietness, and even darkness, of isolation. As we will see in the selected short stories of Porter, Chopin, and Welty, although sometimes isolation leads to total destruction of a character as in the case of "Noon Wine" by Porter, it can also strengthen a character. For instance, in "Old Mortality," it leads Miranda to grow; or it can emancipate a character as will be especially discussed in Chapter 4, "Feminine Independence and Isolation." In this sense, through the examination of isolation in selected short fiction by Chopin, Porter, and Welty, we see that it is not always a negative state in life, but may empower an individual in different ways.

The divisions of chapters in this work are mostly by classification of different aspects of isolation by situational causes: unrequited passion, social elements in communities, poverty, situations in families, feminine independence, and in the last chapter, death. Each type of situation is studied by comparing the differences and similarities among them. For example, Chopin's "Désirée's Baby" and "La Belle Zoraïde" treat isolation imposed on the protagonists by racial discrimination. Their alienation and expulsion from communities are not the results desired and chosen by Désirée and Zoraïde. The same is true with the physically and mentally sterile life of the Mortons in Welty's "The Whistle." On the other hand, some protagonists, especially female characters in the short fiction of the three authors treated in Chapter 4, choose to isolate themselves.

The same was more or less true with the artistic lives of the authors, Porter, Chopin, and Welty, who felt that isolation was a required condition for them in order to create, and out of which they bore the fruits of their fiction. As has been mentioned in the beginning, especially in the life of artists, there is a strong, essential link between isolation and creation. Isolation is not only a physical necessity for the actual process of writing, but also functions as the ultimate source of their thoughts and artistry. In reading through fiction by Porter, Welty, and Chopin, a reader is struck by the richness of the authors' individuality. Only through the writers' inner reflections and inspirations from their solitary thinking were they able to perceive and write about different characters' thoughts and to use their descriptive powers for portraying moods of different times and places.

Louis Forsdale's metaphors comparing isolated human beings and communication between them to islands and bridges between them, in his reworking of John Donne's "Meditation XVII" ("No man is an island . . ."), apply to the significance of creative writing. We can similarly compare writers to isolated islands and their writings to the bridges that they extend to other lands (*Perspectives in Communication* 92.) His passage deliberately reverses Donne's famous lines in which Donne advocates fundamental unions between all human beings. While it describes the relation between isolated human beings and the meaning of communication among them, it conversely reflects on the significance of the separateness between humans and the individuality of each. Applying Forsdale's wording, if writers are isolated islands and their writings are bridges, they create these bridges, their writings, by facing their solitude; that is, by admitting that they are islands and do not merge with others. No genuine individual creation is to be born out of the false illusion of togetherness that can annihilate the power and source of creativity of each individual artist. Lonesomeness can be painful, but talented writers have succeeded in bearing the fruits of their writings by the act of extending bridges from their inner source.

> Every person is an island, isolated from all others in his or her self, forever physically separated after the umbilical cord is cut. The anxiety, the loneliness of the isolation moves us to create bridges between our islands. We extend our hands, fingers touching; we span the distance with our eyes. We speak; we smile. Through such strivings we construct transitory bridges, pathways of signals, that carry delicate freight of meaning. (Forsdale 92)

By going down to the depth inside the self, writers come to grasp the "delicate freight of meaning" in the minds of not only themselves but also others.

They become charged with creativity that can produce "bridges," in Forsdale's terms. Their writing becomes powerful enough to reach down and touch the inner depths in readers and of the characters in the fiction.

In discussing the isolation that writers resort to as the source of their creativity, it should be observed that even the act of extending bridges, that is, the encounter with others, is done through the state of aloneness. Every act by us, of speaking, smiling, and building connections to others does not nullify the fact that each of us is alone.

As has been mentioned, one of the significant reasons a writer needs to go down to the depth of isolation is that isolation inside each self becomes a source of artistry and of materials for writers that will not dry up. Although one of the causes of the occasional pain of isolation is its fathomlessness, the infinity of the state of isolation of each person also becomes for artists a potential that is also immeasurable.

The task of facing isolation is ultimately the task of facing vastness and fathomlessness. The boundlessness of the sea that Edna Pontellier in Chopin's *The Awakening* goes into in order to be ultimately alone represents the infiniteness of isolation. If one tries to see the finite end in solitude, one finds only that there is no end, just as there is no ending border in the sea that Edna merges into. The depth of isolation inside each human being and each writer is also comparable to the infinity of time and space, and of death, in that they are all immeasurable infinity. The implied death in the sea in the ending of *The Awakening* signifies not only the endlessness of the space of the sea but also the endlessness of time, which both symbolize the infinity of space and time of the solitude Edna merges into. To describe the ending of *The Awakening* more plainly, Edna's destiny after her immersion into the sea is completely unknown. Chopin never wrote further about what exactly happens to Edna after she walks into the sea, although it may be obvious that she dies. Her death is the beginning of her journey into the unknown. Neither the author nor readers nor other characters in the book can ever know surely what awaits Edna and what she encounters after her departure from this world.

The various types of isolation treated in each chapter of this book all significantly include the elements of the unknown and the protagonists' encounter with or departure for the unknown. Chopin, Porter, and Welty all endeavor to penetrate into the unknown aspects of human life and psychology, one of which is the extent and nature of solitude and isolation. Although isolation of life and the human mind is pervasive in every aspect and dimension of all kinds of human circumstances, and is, more or less, familiar to everyone, it still remains an ultimate mystery. In the beginning of her article, "The Mysteries of Eudora Welty," Ruth M. Vande Kieft mentions that Welty's writings reveal the writer's concern with the "mystery" of reality. Vande Kieft explains that the term "mystery" used by Welty in her "How I Write" deals with "the enigma of man's being—his relation to the universe; what is secret, concealed, inviolable in any human being, resulting in distance or separation between human beings; the puzzles and difficulties we have about our own feelings, our meaning and our identity" (Vande Kieft 45, Welty 242). Such "puzzles" and "difficulties" even about one's own emotions and thoughts cause one to be isolated not only from others but also from our own selves. One of the most significant emotions analyzed in this book is isolation from one's own self sometimes caused by dishonesty to and deception of oneself or by one's failure to grasp oneself because of, as is mentioned by Vande Kieft, the occasional incredible difficulties of understanding oneself (Vande Kieft 45). Chopin, Porter and Welty all exert themselves to explore the fathomless marsh and mystery of human isolation by means of, and also *because of*, their artistic capability, with their strong inclination to venture into the unknown, the hidden, the neglected, and the enigmatic.

For instance, in "A Memory," one of the short fictions treated in Chapter 2, "Passion and Isolation," Welty uncovers the mysterious depth of an isolated psyche in describing the introverted passion of a schoolgirl. The depth of the author's probe into the girl's mind penetrates into the subconscious of the human mind. Porter's "The Jilting of Granny Weatherall" is also an attempt to study and exhibit the perplexing enigma of the inner mind of an isolated person, i.e., of a dying elderly woman "jilted" in her youth. It is also the writer's undertaking to observe, analyze, and to present the threshold between life and death and the beginning of death, one of the ultimate mysteries in the universe along with its antithesis, life. In her "Flowering Judas" Porter also ventures to explicate the entangled subconscious of a female survivor who is dreadfully puzzled and stricken by a guilty conscience concerning her comrade's death. In Chopin's "Caline" the author narrates the inward passion of a country girl which would have remained unseen had it not been for the perspective the author provides, her covert sentiment for a young man whom she only encountered accidentally and whose track she totally loses.

As will be studied in Chapter 3, "Family and Isolation," "Flowers for Marjorie," and "A Curtain of Green" by Welty all concern psychic isolations of the characters in their situations in families. They deal with the connection among domestic predicaments, consequent psychological troubles of the characters and the mystery of death. Chapter 6 sums up the way Chopin, Porter, and Welty unfold the image of death in their short fiction as the culminating form of isolation, separation, and mystery.

Other short fictions that are to be studied in this book include the following selections. For Chapter 2, "Passion and Isolation," "At the Landing" is selected from Welty's short stories. Chopin's "A Visit to Avoyelles," "Madame Célestin's Divorce" and "A Lady of Bayou St. John" are the stories of how men's passion for women can be unrequited, and which end in the revelation of how false their hopes were. In her "A Shameful Affair," "A Respectable Woman," and "The Kiss," Chopin narrates how a moral sense or pride constrains women from being honest with their own emotions and desires.

Chapter 4, "Feminine Independence and Isolation," is a study of another significant pattern of isolation, the linking and conflicting patterns between female independence and isolation. In the case of women's isolation, as will be examined in this chapter, women sometimes prefer isolation when they try to remove constraints imposed upon them within family or domestic protections and confinements. The short stories by the three authors treated in this chapter, however, reveal that the pattern is not simple. The female characters' trials in their self-emancipation do not necessarily result simply in their triumph in complete independence. In fact, one of the categories of this group dealing with the relation between women's independence and their isolation reveals the pictures of their failures in their attempts at self-emancipation. However, many of the stories dealing with women's failures in securing independence are not simple portrayals of their total failures. We have seen that the stories that describe successful cases of freedom and independence do not simplistically present bliss without a speck of trouble, either.

The selection of Chopin's short stories abounds in sketches of women torn between independence and their need to belong. Such portrayals are enough to prove Chopin's insightful awareness of people's conflicting and alternating needs to have companionship with others and to keep one's self-reliance. "The Story of an Hour," "Elizabeth Stock's One Story," and *The Awakening* all end in the death of the female protagonists, but whether or not death is their complete defeat is open to discussion. "Elizabeth Stock's One Story" and "Miss McEnders" both disclose the pathos of women's ignorance of the world, which, however, is not necessarily entirely their own fault, but is one of the outcomes of a male-dominated social structure. Chopin's "Beyond the Bayou" and "A Pair of Silk Stockings" can be analyzed as presenting some rays of hopefulness among other stories with darker conclusions, although the women's achievements in them may be minor and feeble. "The Maid of Saint Philippe" will also be mentioned. The discussion in the chapter will also touch upon her "Emancipation: Life Fable," which allegorically narrates the process and significance of emancipation.

In some of Porter's short stories we also see an emphasis on women's independence, as in "Old Mortality," a story of a growing girl's departure for the world outside the circle of her relatives and family members, and "The Last Leaf," narrating the resolve of an old slave woman to be by herself for the first time in her life and for good. In the analysis of Porter's short fiction concerning women's independence and their isolation, some cross-referential discussion will be made to "The Jilting of Granny Weatherall" and "María Concepción," examined in the second and third chapter, respectively, about heterosexual relationships. The purpose of such discussion is to reinforce the point that women's frustration over men whom they take as ineffectual or unreliable, which is often one of Porter's themes, can sometimes cause a woman to choose independence over companionship with a man, at the cost of isolation.

Welty was rather resentful of the women's rights movement (*Conversations with Eudora Welty*, 36, 135-36) and women in her short stories do not insist on their independence and freedom *per se*. However, we still see that women characters in her short fiction also experience isolation as a result, for instance, of the social conventions that require women and men to play rigorously limited roles in limited situations. On this point, "Flowers for Marjorie" and "A Curtain of

Green," which are examined in the third chapter, "Family and Isolation," will be discussed again.

Chapter 5, "Social Issues and Isolation," discusses the relation between social issues and human isolation. From Chopin's short fiction, the two stories that treat the issue of racial discrimination will be mentioned. In "Désirée's Baby" the community and a spouse expel the female protagonist, Désirée, on the ground that she is found to be nonwhite, only to discover later that the accusation is false. In "La Belle Zoraïde" the community deprives Zoraïde of two loves, the mental torture of which soon causes her incurable insanity. In these two stories by Chopin, actual historical and sociological factors of the periods constitute the background of the isolated circumstances and psychology of the protagonists.

Some stories by Welty and Porter depict how poverty can separate people and cause them to be isolated. Welty's "The Whistle" and Porter's "He" address the stark predicaments of poor whites. Chapter 6 sums up the analysis of isolation and separation in the foregoing chapters by interpreting the meaning of symbolic death that readers find in the different forms of isolation treated previously. The chapter intends to probe the nature and meaning of death as the final culmination of isolation. Some stories describe death as an occurrence, and descriptions in other stories try to cross the boundary between life and death and to see beyond. When readers read through the short stories of the three authors, they not only find that the theme of isolation runs through a large portion of them, but also that in a deeper level of this theme, the image of death significantly hovers here and there. These observations that readers can make about these short stories is one of the indications that the undercurrent of all human conditions is not only isolation, but also death. Forsdale's passage about human communication compares death with the terminating disintegration of the links built between isolated individuals. In the middle of the passage, after he suggests the comparison of such links to bridges, he goes on to conclude it with the metaphor of the final fall of the bridge with death:

> In fair weather the bridges hold, in foul weather they collapse. We work a lifetime keeping the bridges open between our personal islands. The tolling bell signals the death of an island, the collapse of a bridge, punctuating the eternal state of isolation that we endure, seeking always to alleviate. (92)

Among the short stories by Chopin, Porter, and Welty, the ones that are commonly considered most significant treat death in one way or the other, such as Chopin's *The Awakening*, Porter's "Flowering Judas," and Welty's "Death of a Traveling Salesman." The sixth chapter discusses again the stories that will have already been discussed in former chapters in their connection with the theme of isolation observed from the viewpoints of various differing situational factors, so as to focus on the theme of death as final isolation.

The nature and the extent of isolation that will be observed in this book vary by means of divisions of chapters. But one of the common traits that readers find in the short fiction of Chopin, Porter, and Welty is that many of the circumstances in them are found in the lives of ordinary people. By contrasting Welty's characters with those in many other Southern fictions and dramas, Reynolds Price shows that they are not extraordinary in appearance, speech, and action, at least on the surface (77). He points out that Welty's characters are not "freaks" as are those of McCullers, O'Connor, and other Southern writers, although they are predominantly and importantly outsiders (77). Similar observation can be made about the characters in the works of Porter and Chopin. Therefore, one main thread of this book is to plumb the psychological level and see through the hidden enigma that is beneath the daily lives of ordinary people. Another significant thread is to analyze the pattern of destruction of the ordinary lives of ordinary citizens by social factors, which at times intertwine with the underlying psychological factors of characters that would otherwise have remained unseen and untouched. In this sense, this study is an analysis of both inner and outer facets of people's lives delineated by Chopin, Porter, and Welty in their short fiction. Its central and comprehensive focus is on the theme of isolation, which the author finds to be a major facet of the works and lives of the three authors, and above all, of the human condition.

Notes

1. Elaine Showalter quotes Guy de Maupassant's "Solitude" in the beginning of her article, "Tradition and the Female Talent: *The Awakening* as a Solitary Book" (Showalter 33). She indicates in her note to the passage that it was quoted in Margaret Culley's "Edna Pontellier: 'A Solitary Soul,'" in *The Awakening*, Norton Critical Edition, 1976. Guy de Maupassant, "Solitude," trans. Kate Chopin, *St. Louis Life* 12 (December 28, 1895,) 30 (Culley 224-25, Showalter 55).

Chapter 2

Passion and Isolation

In Welty's "At the Landing" the female protagonist, Jenny Lockhart, feels that it is ultimately impossible for her to merge with Billy Floyd, the man she loves. She compares the impossibility for an individual to unite with the central core of the existence of another with waves that can only approach the shore of an island: "if there were an island out in the sea, the waves at its shore would never come over the place in the middle of the island" (*The Wide Net and Other Stories* 209). Bridges can extend from the shore of an island to that of another isle, but they cannot alter the fundamental separateness between islands, and cannot put them together, no matter how firmly they are built. The metaphor quoted above is preceded by two others that both describe the inviolability of the heart of one person:

> She looked at the lump of amber, and looked through to its core. Nobody could ever know about the difference between the radiance that was the surface and the radiance that was inside. There were the two worlds. There was no way at all to put a finger on the center of light. And if there were a mountain, the cloud over it could not touch its heart when it traveled over. (209)

What Jenny sees in the unapproachable composure of Billy Floyd is not simply his rejection of her in their male-female relationship, but is also the representation of existential separateness between any two humans. She remembers that when she tried to reach him, he "turned away—not from her, but toward something" (209). She wonders: "Was it toward one thing, toward some one thing alone?" (209). The direct answer to Jenny's query on the direction of Billy's inward motive is not given. However, the speculation that Jenny makes on the nature of her love for Billy that follows the metaphors cited above implies that both love of one for another and inviolability of an individual are manifold rather than directed toward "one thing alone."

> But it was when love was of the one for the one, that it seemed to hold all that was multitudinous and nothing was single any more. She had one love and that was all, but she dreamed that she lined up on both sides of the road to see her love come by in a procession. She herself was more people than there were people in The Landing, and her love was enough to pass through the whole night, never lifting the same face. (209-10)

Both Billy Floyd's identity and Jenny's love for him have many facets rather than only one aspect. This is one of the indications that inside each person there is an immeasurable expanse that holds countless possibilities, each of which cannot be simplistically pinned down.

The way Welty writes about this situation makes a reader sense that Jenny is not necessarily resentful in experiencing this realization. As in many other short stories by Welty, despite the violent events that take place, a large portion of "At the Landing" centers on the patterns of Jenny's inner reflections.[1] It is true that readers find a great disparity between the brutality of the actions and the philosophical composure Jenny reaches in the middle of the story in her reflection on love. She is raped by Billy, consequently deserted by him callously, and is further raped by several other men. Yet in the middle of the story we see that she almost affirms her love for Billy. She comes to this affirmation, apparently not because her love for him has been reciprocated, but through her insight into the existential separateness between herself and another. The way Jenny's praise of love is preceded by the descriptive metaphors of separateness shows that one of the author's views on isolation is that she perceives it and love as inseparable conditions of human hearts and relations.

However, in "At the Landing," the violation of Jenny, especially by several river fishermen, leaves quite an impression of savageness, and subsequently, some sense of confusion concerning the consistency of the fiction.[2] It is rather difficult to come to the satisfactory understanding of the meaning of the smile on her face at the end of the story after the barbarous treatment of her as a river prostitute by fishermen. In her relation with Billy, it is not entirely impossible to see that Jenny's character grows through her love for him, her physical relation with him, and his departure from her and The Landing, although some brutal elements are involved. However, Louise Westling does not think of Jenny's smile after the gang rape as a hopeful ray (84). He writes that Welty deliberately made the ending of "At the Landing" ambiguous (84). To interpret her smile at the end of the fiction as the result of her growth and her subsequent acquired capability of the complete acceptance of any harsh reality seems like too much of a masochistic interpretation and an insult to feminine sexuality. Is this ending an indictment of Billy's abandonment of her? Does it intend to say that if Billy had not forsaken her, she would not have been placed in such a plight? Westling mentions that the description of her smile is like a last ray in a dying sky that makes us fear that her life disappears just as the last light in the sky (84).

One interpretation of the savageness of the ending of "At the Landing" is that it expresses the futility as well as the violent effect of sexuality. As Westling interprets, the flooding river and sexual force of Billy Floyd are equated in the work (Westling 84). However, such vital forces do not bring about a wholesome union between Billy and Jenny. Her sexual relation with him is only a physical consummation and does not lead to their further mental communication, although he saves her life when the flood comes.

Another Welty short story, "Livvie," also handles forceful male sexuality of a Dionysian protagonist. Again it is not certain whether the union with male sexuality mentally frees the female protagonist and whether it becomes the solution to her isolation, either, although the ending of "Livvie" is much more hopeful than that of "At the Landing." The ending of "Livvie" is open, and Livvie's fate after the ending is left to readers' speculation.

"At the Landing" and "A Memory," also by Welty, have some essential elements in common, the most significant of which concerning the theme of isolation. In both stories the female protagonists are aware of the inviolable isolation of the men they love as well as of their own solitariness. Jenny and the schoolgirl in "A Memory" are both isolated people in that their loves are not requited, that they do not get to speak to the men they love, and that they do not commune with other members in the story, either. However, they not only peer into their own solitude, but also, through their observant, apprehensive, and introverted dispositions, see how solitary the men, Billy and the boy, are. What they see through in the inapproachable solitude of the men they love when they come to terms with it is the "innocence" and "mystery" of the hearts of these men, and they both feel somewhat protective of what they see as the men's vulnerability (*Wide Net* 186, 189). In "At the Landing" Jenny beholds his innocence as she feels that her own innocence leaves her since she has begun to love him. Watching him in the woods, Jenny realizes: "As she was living and inviolate, so of course was he" and acknowledges that "a fragile mystery was in everyone and in herself, since there it was in Floyd, and that whatever she did, she would be bound to ride over and hurt" (188-89). In her dreams, she sees that he is "safe and deep in his innocence, safe and away from the outside, deeper than quiet" (209).

In "A Memory," "I," a schoolgirl, is as much fearful of any danger that might befall the boy she loves as she is sensitively alarmed by anything else (*A Curtain of Green and Other Stories* 147-57). She is constantly apprehensive of any potential peril that she imagines can assail him. She observes "unconcern and even stupidity" on the boy's face, but his innocent unawareness of the latent dangers of the world only adds to her intense concern for him because she feels "a mystery deeper than danger which hung about him" (150-51). The last sentence of "A Memory" condenses what the girl observes in him and how she feels about him as she imagines going back to school. "I could even foresee the way he would stare back, speechless and innocent, a medium-sized boy with blond hair, his unconscious eyes looking beyond me and out the window, solitary and unprotected" (157). The way the boy is alone and prone to vulnerability is, in the eyes of the girl, almost existential because, in her view, his self is beyond her wish to reach and protect him, and furthermore, beyond everything else just as his eyes unconsciously travel out the window yonder.

The awareness of Jenny and the schoolgirl of the lonesomeness of another individual whom they happen to love, as well as of their own isolation, brings them to a mental state that verges on a "dream," or conversely, is brought to them through such a state in both stories. In "A Memory" the schoolgirl constantly goes back and forth between the repugnant vulgarity of reality that she sees on the beach and the dream world she cherishes. She never stops thinking about the boy and repeatedly recalls the moment of having accidentally touched the boy's wrist on the stairs at school. She feels that thinking of the boy she loves in dreams not only makes her full of apprehension of what might happen to the boy but also redeems the orderliness and beauty of the universe that she always tries to construct and keep intact in her mind. She considers going back to reality as a departure from the shelter of her personal dream world: as she goes back to reality she says that she "emerged again from the protection of my dream" (156). However, for "I" of "A Memory" dreaming is an active state she places herself in rather than a passive state an outside force drives her into. She resolutely speaks of her dream world that is plain but genuine. She herself intends to be a determined and stern keeper of the complete harmony of this cosmos as its creator, although she eventually reaches the realization that the order of that cosmos can be breached.[3] The motif of dream as nourishment of love in "At the Landing" is not an active posture of the female protagonist as it is in "A Memory." It is more grounded on the scenes and seasons of the place, The Landing, and conforms to Welty's statement previously referred to that she was trying to express the sense of lostness and enchantment of the place. The Landing is portrayed as evoking dream all through the seasons. In spring, it lies in "golden haze," and through the haze a man carrying a fishing pole walks to the river "like a dreamer" (*Wide Net* 180). In the beginning of her love, while Jenny watches Billy riding in a pasture, herself sitting on a stile in a graveyard, she feels "as if she were dreaming" as he comes toward her (185). After she is saved from the flood by him, violated by him, and yet realizes that her wish cannot be fulfilled, she thinks of love in terms of dream as she watches the moon rise above "The Landing." "The dream of love" remains only a dream, but she is still convinced that there is "a country" that it leads to, and compares it with the moon that has risen (202). "There was a need in all dreams for something to stay far, far away, never to torment with the rest, and the bright moon now was that" (202). At this point, Jenny feels that the sight of the moon somewhat cures her sorrow as it enables her to regard love as dream.

After Billy has departed The Landing, Jenny starts on a journey for the quest of love "in the dream of July," in which she feels that again she knows so little of love and is lost (211). The mood of the season of the place is vividly portrayed and captured in the imagery of dream:

> It was July when Jenny left The Landing. The grass was tall and gently ticking between the tracks of the road. The stupor of air, the quiet of the river that now went behind a veil, the sheen of heat and the gray sheen of summering trees, and the silence of day and night seemed all to touch, to bathe and administer to The Landing. The little town took a languor and a kind of beauty from the treatment of time and place. It stretched and swooned, and when two growing boys knelt in the road and caught the sun rays in a bit of glass and got fire, they seemed to tease a sleeper, and when they said "Hooray!" they sounded like adventurers in a dream. (210)

The author continues to describe in detail how small creatures and plants respond to the atmosphere of the languor and add to it. Just as everything is in stupor in the season in the place, the clarity of the meaning of her relationship with Billy Floyd is lost to Jenny again, although she may have known something about him before; "and now once more, in the dream of July, she knew very little, she was lost in wonder again" (211).

As Jenny is about to depart on her lonely journey, the day is about to end. Again plants and creatures all respond to the closing of the day, as if to accentuate Jenny's departure that is without clear destination. Jenny looks behind at the house she is leaving. In the evening in the summer it exudes some beauty, as if to heighten Jenny's daring and lonely choice. As Jenny begins to walk, the creatures and plants of the place actually begin to enfold her. Nature in the scene symbolizes the endless nature of Jenny's wandering from which she cannot escape.

> Then green branches closed it over, and with her next step trumpet and muscadine vines and the great big-leaved vines made pillars about the trunks of the trees and arches and buttresses all among them. Passion flowers bloomed with their white and purple rays about her shoulders and under her feet. She walked on into the streaming hot shade of the wilderness, and put out her hands between the hanging vines. She feared the snakes in the sudden cool. Like thousands of silver bells the frogs rang her through the swamp, which then closed behind her. (212)

Although Jenny eventually reaches the river, the river is not her final destination. Everything there is also blurry, dim, languorous, and even suggests despair: "All things, river, sky, fire, and air, seemed the same color, the color that is seen behind the closed eyelids, the color of day when vision and despair are the same thing" (212).

In both "At the Landing" and "A Memory," Jenny and "I" cannot communicate with Billy and the boy, respectively. The lack, or complete blockage, of communication between a male and a female is commonly characteristic of the two stories. Sexual relation is without any verbal communication in "At the Landing." The pure monologue of the first person narrator is without any sign of the possibility of communication between the boy and "I." When Jenny tries to confess her emotions, after she is saved from the flood by Billy, twice her words are stopped by his frowns. The schoolgirl in "A Memory" never gets to exchange a single word with the boy and only cherishes her love for him inside herself. We find a similar situation in Chopin's "Caline" where the female character cannot find a channel of communication with the young man she cherishes. A country girl begins to love a youth she accidentally meets, but never gets to see him, never gets a chance to talk to him again, and completely loses track of him. Caline's one-sided emotion for the youth is more passive than that of the schoolgirl in "A Memory." It is, in one sense, more one-sided and passive than that of Jenny, too, although no sexual violence takes place in "Caline." The only time Caline sees the youth is when he makes a sketch of her when a train stops by accident in the middle of the countryside. It only stops for a short time and he is on the train again before finishing the sketch. Although Caline sets out to live in a city to seek him, she realizes that she has been left no clue to his whereabouts and that she cannot even find out his name. In being made to face this fact, all Caline does is to cry alone, not being consoled or seen by anybody. Although there is no philosophical speculation on the part of Caline on aloneness and the pain of love, the story of Caline is, in a sense, hopeless and poignant as a case of one-sided emotion. Just as sexual relations and saving Jenny's life do not mean much to Billy, the youth completely forgets having met and sketched Caline.

Till the end, the story appears to be about the contact and contrast between city life and country life. But in the end, it turns out to be about a completely unreciprocated emotion of a young woman for a young man and the transience of relations between people in the rushing passage of life. In the beginning of the story, symbolically, Caline is awakened by an outside element suddenly coming into her peaceful country life as she is awakened from her lazy and relaxed slumber as the train suddenly stops in the middle of the open field. The description of the beginning of this happening tells us that in the first place the novel incident is no little shock for the young woman: "She had slept long and soundly, when something awoke her as suddenly as if it had been a blow" (246). It tells that "such a thing had not happened before within her recollection" (246). Caline attempts to overcome the shock of her first exposure to new elements by actually approaching nearer to what has been introduced to her by accident. She ventures to get clearer knowledge about the original departing point and destination of the train cargoes and bravely sets off to live in the city. In the city, after some effort, it seems to her that perhaps she has succeeded in merging with city life because many things in the city start to appear quite agreeable to her. It has not been difficult for her to adjust and accept the surface features of the life she has never known before, such as being exposed to the language used in the city and going about a market place and a seaport.

However, what really happened in her heart is subtler than outward factors. Pretty soon, she reaches a truer realization about what the experience has caused in her mind. After she has gotten used to the physical novelties of the city, she faces the void in her mind. She comes to see that she has ultimately failed to fill the desire of her heart, that is, to meet and to talk to the pleasant-faced boy who had made the sketch of her that day in the countryside. For Caline the encounter with city life becomes the initiation to a new experience of feeling hurt. In finding where trains go, traveling there, and actually living there, she might have been vaguely, and as it turns out, falsely, hoping that such efforts on her side have been actually bridging the distance between the boy and her, only to find out that they were vain. She is forced to accept the hard fact that their encounter in the country was only transient. The trouble she took to see the youth again are efforts to approach him by going closer to physical realities that surround him and that to her seemed to be parts of him. Although it has not been impossible for her to fuse with them, she must realize that blending with what seemed to surround and constitute his life does not allow her to fuse with his own personality. Caline has been able to approach the shore of the island that is comparable to the surface factors about the youth, but cannot fill the core of her wish, that is, to meet him in person and to reach his self deeper in the center of the island.

Quite a few short stories by Chopin treat the futility and pain of one-sided emotion in men-women relationships. Her "A Visit to Avoyelles," "Madame Célestin's Divorce," and "A Lady of Bayou St. John" are all about unrequited passion of men for women. Each of these short stories gives somewhat comic and thus pathetic portraits of men who, in the end, all suffer from the hard realization that their hopes have been false. In all of them, their passion for young wives is flamed by hopes because, at least in the eyes of these men, there appear to be enough reasons for the wives to want to leave their present marital ties and come to these men. Mentine in "A Visit to Avoyelles" is said to have been suffering from difficult and poor living conditions in her marriage to Jules. Célestin, Madame Célestin's husband, is prone to drinking, leads a dissipating life, and neglects his family. Gustave, husband of Madame Delisle, a lady of Bayou St. John, is simply not present at home, being away in the war. In each story, objective readers and the male characters see in the end how one-sided and false the men's passion, hopes, and dreams have been. But till the revelation to the contrary, these men keep allowing their emotions to flame up in their minds. They continue to eagerly plan and dream of a rosy future for them and the women they love, being undoubtedly convinced that the wives are certainly dreaming and planning the same. In their imagination they are united happily with the young wives they love, although such unions take place only in their illusions. Doudouce in "A Visit to Avoyelles" actually dreams in his sleep that Mentine sees him "with appealing eyes" to "rescue" her (229). Lawyer Paxton in "Madame Célestin's Divorce" is portrayed as being in "a stupid habit of dreaming" (278). The passage strongly emphasizes that he dreams about marrying Madame Célestin. Sépincourt in "A Lady of Bayou St. John" even succeeds in winning a whisper of consent to his passionate entreaty from a docile, delicate and fragile-hearted lady, which only works to consolidate his wishful conviction.

Contrary to what each man comes to believe in his own mind in stretching the imagination, in the end, the women characters do not harbor the same plan of eloping as the men do. The reality turns out to be much more twisted than what the men imagined initially. Their shock in being shown the conclusion is not little because for some time it has seemed hopeful that their relation with the women would develop in the direction of their wish. Mentine, Madame Célestin, and Madame Delisle all appear as dainty, obedient, and frail females who, from the men's vantage point, will easily and naturally fall to the romantic and earnest courting of other men who are not their husbands. But the tenacity the women show in the end quite bewilders and disappoints them. In the men's disillusionment and bitter realization of reality, readers see typical examples of thwarted hopes of romantic unions and of unbridgeable discrepancy between what a man and a woman tend to think and hope concerning the relation between them. Although these short stories by Chopin may seem common and superficial, they are *triste* and apt sketches of isolation of individuals who happen to be placed outside certain unions, in these cases, outside the marital bonds the young wives are in, and who fail to break the bonds of the unions in order to win love. As Sépincourt of "A Lady of Bayou St. John" bitterly contemplates in the end that it is hard for him to "comprehend that psychological enigma, a woman's heart," at the end of each story, a heart of one individual becomes and remains an "enigma" for another (302).

In Chopin's "A Shameful Affair," "A Respectable Woman," and "The Kiss," we find a similar, yet slightly different pattern of unfulfilled emotion and isolation. As in the stories by Chopin discussed so far, in these three stories, the passions of the protagonists, Mildred Orme in "A Shameful Affair," Mrs. Baroda in "A Respectable Woman," and Nathalie in "The Kiss," are not satisfied. However, unlike Caline and the men in the previous three stories, forgotten and ignored by a man or woman they feel for, Mildred, Mrs. Baroda, and Nathalie choose more or less of their own accord not to let their emotions become known to others. In their cases, the men for whom they feel desire may have reciprocated their passion if they had chosen to act towards the further fulfillment of the relationships. In this sense their choices not to let the relationships go further are similar to those by Madame Célestin and Madame Delisle in the previous three stories. Just as they have the practical sense and knowledge that it is more advantageous for them, as women living in a society, to stick to their current roles, Mildred, Mrs. Baroda, and Nathalie choose what they think benefits them more than totally unreined surrender to the untimely passion that seizes them. However, the dispositions and the nature of the motives of Mildred, Mrs. Baroda, and Nathalie are not the same as those of Mentine, Madame Célestin and Madame Delisle. Mentine, Madame Célestin, and Madame Delisle are very passive women both in their pride and their awareness of relationships. Mildred, Mrs. Baroda and Nathalie are portrayed as much more proud women than the three wives. Even if six of them may all be proud, Mentine, Madame Célestin, and Madame Delisle are not as conscious of their pride as Mildred, Mrs. Baroda, and Nathalie. Mentine, Madame Célestin, and Madame Delisle are much less aware of what goes on between them and a former friend, a confidant, and a neighbor, respectively, than Mildred, Mrs. Baroda, and Nathalie are of the passion aroused in their hearts. Being far more aware of both their own pride and their emotion for the men they have relations with than Mentine, Madame Célestin, and Madame Delisle are, they are more torn between the two conflicting desires in their own minds than the three wives. In order to make their social aspiration win over an emotion that is as strong as, or stronger than, their need for social esteem, they deliberately and rashly deny the passion in their own hearts, regarding it as undesirable and "shameful." In following their social sense of restraint rather than their hearts' inner desires, they are separated from their own inner selves, which is one of the most fundamental forms of isolation. They decide that they are more concerned about what other people think of them rather than what they really want, and choose not to face and not to come to terms with their true selves. This does not mean, however, that they are self-effacing. Rather, what makes them want to adhere to social decorum is their strong ego and pride. "A Shameful Affair," "A Respectable Woman," and "The Kiss" all reveal and explicate to readers what is beneath the "respectable" veneer of the three women. The stories considerably incorporate their viewpoints, whereas "A Visit to Avoyelles," "Madame Célestin's Divorce," and "Lady of Bayou St. John" present the viewpoints of the three men who are in love with the young wives.

Martin Simpson repeatedly uses the term, "isolated," in his article, "Chopin's 'A Shameful Affair,'" to explain how Mildred Orme isolates herself from relationships in the city in order to shut out possible sources of emotional disturbance. In doing so, she isolates herself from her own active sensuality. She feels that she must act with sufficient "dignity" to a farmhand so as to "define her position toward him" (133). She would not want to succumb to her own "shameful whim," which she feels assails her heart "like an ugly dream" (135). Meanwhile, Mildred's determined plan to remain lofty with "her Browning or her Ibsen" has not arisen from her inner intellectual and emotional drives, and does not enhance her thoughts and insights into life, relationships, emotions, and sexuality (131). Instead of being enriched through exposure to the wealth of the vast emotional and cultural varieties that literature presents, she uses it to isolate herself from emotions, and impoverishes herself by confining herself to what she believes is a higher plane. That she feels "idle" and "piqued" while at the farmhouse with the books proves that she does not read and appreciate literary works but that she only carries them around as symbols of status (132). The isolated fortress into which she escapes does not help her cope with her problems. Rather, her attempt at escape makes her even more vulnerable and reveals her weakness more than before. In trying to completely shut out nuisances, she has failed to acquire immunity against them and emotional flexibility to deal with them. She grows susceptible to such a minor trigger as having a piece of paper she drops at a door picked up by one of the working men of the farm. She yields quite impulsively to sexual temptation when such a moment comes, and later regrets her action to the extreme of detesting herself.

The rigid reaction Mildred takes against her own sexuality can be similarly observed in the behavior of Mrs. Baroda. Like Mildred, she refuses to admit to herself that she is attracted to a man whose charm her prestigious position as a wife of a wealthy man does not permit her to yield to. She will have to compromise her pride merely to acknowledge attraction. The more she is drawn to Gouvernail, her husband's friend, the further she turns herself away from him. She also would not confide in her husband, whom she feels is also her friend, of what she regards as "folly" that has been aroused in her heart (336). Such restraint as a sensible and "respectable" woman, however, leaves her rather confused instead of making her life stable and calm as she aims to make it (336). All she is able to do about it is to abruptly leave the source of her bewilderment, just as all Mildred does after being disturbed while in the city is to escape by going to an isolated farm.

Nathalie in "The Kiss" does her best to cover up the undesirable passion for Harvy by way of telling Brantain that Harvy's intimate behavior toward her is only an expression of sibling-like feeling, so as not to lose Brantain whose wealth she craves to possess by marrying him. She does not realize till the end of the story that the choice she makes to secure Brantain's fortune in agreeing to become his wife inevitably makes it impossible for her to fulfill the passion between her and Harvy. She is not only proud in wanting to be married to a wealthy man of a social rank, but also vain and confident of her own attractiveness as a woman. She is also wrongly confident of her own cleverness in making maneuvers between the two men and calculating and using their emotions to her advantage. Until Harvy refuses to have further relations with her after the wedding, she continues to believe that her clever maneuvers combined with her charm will make both Brantain and Harvy act as she wants them to and let her satisfy both her desire for money and her passion. She feels "like a chess player, who, by the clever handling of his pieces, sees the game taking the course intended" (381). Contrary to what she thinks of her own move, the comment she makes to Brantain about her relationship with Harvy is rather clumsy. Although Brantain guilelessly takes her remark seriously and believes her, being driven by his wishful hope, in an objective observation, the way Nathalie and Harvy act with each other is obviously beyond mere brotherly affection. Without realizing Brantain's presence, Harvy has amorously kissed her when Brantain unexpectedly comes into the room, whose atmosphere was romantic and murky enough even for shy and unattractive Brantain to be in a mood to dare confess his emotion and propose to Nathalie. "It was still quite light out of doors, but inside with the curtains drawn and the smouldering fire sending out a dim uncertain glow, the room was full of deep shadow" (379). When the incident takes place, she is taken aback because she fails to resist Harvy's kiss instantly. She dares not attempt to give an explanation to Brantain for fear that she might further reveal what she does not want him to know, her passion for Harvy, which she finds quite difficult to do away with. Nathalie's rather crude tactics work with Brantain, and she has him and his money, as the author puts it, but her moves offend Harvy considerably, especially when he hears from Brantain after the wedding of the explanation she has given Brantain about her relationship with Harvy. Harvy says to Nathalie condescendingly, smiling, "I don't know what you've been telling him," and makes it clear to her that he will not even let her kiss him. The author concludes the story with a touch of humor: "Well, she had Brantain and his million left. A person can't have everything in this world; and it was a little unreasonable of her to expect it" (381).

What Mildred, Mrs. Baroda, and Nathalie experience in these stories is also experienced by one of the most illustrious characters, Laura, in "Flowering Judas" by Porter. However, Laura's circumstances are much more complicated than those of Mildred, Mrs. Baroda, and Nathalie. As the result of choosing worldly merits Laura also experiences isolation and what James T. F. Tanner describes as "a conflict between loyalty to the world and loyalty to the spirit" in his interpretation of "Flowering Judas" (Tanner 143). In the case of Mildred and Nathalie in Chopin's two short stories, what causes them to want to retain worldly status is mainly their vanity. For Laura, by the time the story takes place, her struggle to keep her place in the given situation involves strategies for mere survival, although she may not be entirely free from vanity. Like other comrades trapped in dark alleys for whom she carries messages and other daily necessities, Laura is now dependent on the objectionable Braggioni for earning a living. Although she is quite unwilling to respond to his desire for her and keeps a rigid posture while he serenades and mocks her, at the same time, she tactfully and carefully manages not to offend him for fear of losing income. She is aware of the risk of offending him. No one, including herself, dares to oppose him and to fight to regain justice and fairness.

Just as Mildred, Mrs. Baroda, and Nathalie grow confused as the result of their inability to face their inner amorous drives, Laura is a very confused character, unable to come to terms with what her intuition tells her, to act according to that intuition, and to sort out situations. M. M. Liberman refers to Porter's own comments on the story and emphasizes that readers are able to see the extremely complex layers of Laura's mind through Porter's perfect narrative (56). In what the author tells of the story in *Katherine Anne Porter: Conversations*, we hear another of the author's frank remarks about what a perplexed individual she attempted to portray. Porter speaks of the same girl reminiscing that she was unable to manage herself, because she could not deal with her own nature and feared everything (90). One of the main reasons that Laura's dilemma is particularly complicated is that Braggioni, the man she detests at heart, is supposedly a leader of an idealistic cause. Initially, to serve him by running his errands meant for her an act of supporting and actively working for the noble cause. However, by the time of the narration, he has become an unidealistic character while slyly keeping the false mask of humanitarian idealism and kindness, and she finds herself trapped. Although Laura has already discerned Braggioni's falsity, in actuality she continues to be closer to him than to other comrades, which is exactly the goal of his schemes.

Needless to say, Braggioni is a central representation of many of the undesirable elements in the political revolution narrated in "Flowering Judas."[4] In the story any genuine element of human passion either for a noble cause or for others has been lost, distorted, and brought down to the unidealistic level of either exploiting others through machinations or of detestable forms of self-indulgence. That is the reason cynicism and disillusionment pervade the whole story, as critics discussing "Flowering Judas" have generally observed. In such a situation so devoid of hope and any other positive element, characters are all isolated from one another. Braggioni, now leading a life of using others either for political and economical schemes or for the pleasure of fulfilling his own worldly desires, has completely given up keeping his spiritual integrity in the struggle that anybody generally goes through between one's worldly desires and spiritual integrity. As Robert H. Brinkmeyer, Jr. notes critically, because of the manner of living he has now chosen to live, he fails to have a true bond with anybody and is spiritually isolated (76-77). The nature of the failure of his relationships with others is especially conspicuous in his treatment of and relationships with women, particularly with his own wife and Laura. Observing his behavior toward his wife and Laura, one might think, or Braggioni himself might think, that he is a man of genuine passion and compassion. It may be true that these two women are the only people around him to whom he openly shows his emotions and opinions. Being hard-hearted and calculating, Braggioni sees other males basically as business associates, whom he values only in terms of profits he can get from them, whereas he feels that he can be honest only with women, especially with his wife and Laura. Precisely because of this reason, the disagreeable traits of his character and thinking become least disguised in his relationships with these two women and in what he shows and tells them. It is rather obvious that his chief approach to women is to be condescending with them when one observes what he expects from and how he acts with the two, and what he tells them about women.

His wife is the only person with whom he acts with a seemingly uncalculating abandon of emotion, as we see in his way of crying with her. However, the relationship between them and his treatment of her is solely based on his abuse of her emotion, and thus the spousal passion between them is not as genuine as he deceitfully contrives for others to believe. The way his wife kneels, unlaces his shoes, and washes his feet without blaming him, though with a sad expression, after his frequent and prolonged absences and his habitual fornication with other women is the utter subjugation of her self. The reason why he can act with her without any emotional restraint is that he has managed to form her habits so as to make her totally serve him and his convenience while making her entirely sacrifice herself. Why she obeys him in such a way is a subject of discussion of women's issues, and will be mentioned again in chapter 5, "Female Independence and Isolation." But on Braggioni's part, his treatment of his wife most clearly shows, when compared to any other relationships he forms with any other individual, that he values relationships only in proportion to the freedom he is allowed by the other party to limitlessly pursue his self-indulgence. With him, the angelic attitude of his wife in her masochistic attempt to entirely forgive him without any sign of rebuke does not function to make him regret. Rather it adds another item to the list of the various forms of self-love he engages in, in the case of his wife, that of the cathartic pleasure of shedding tears with her and going through the act of being forgiven and forgiving. Such a scene between Braggioni and his wife has become ritualized; that is, especially for Braggioni, it is completely void of its initial significance of real forgiving and regretting, and has become an act of habit between them without any effect for the actual betterment of their relationship. Still, they repeat the same rite indefinitely. So long as Braggioni remains as completely uninterested as he is in what life is like for her, or for any other person other than himself, he will continue to take advantage of whatever available measures to ensure his own physical and emotional welfare. He is completely unaware, or blinds his awareness on purpose, of the fact that his partner's, i.e., his wife's, view of the situation between them might be completely different from what he adamantly intends to keep it to be. In this sense his notion of the nature of the marital relation between the two is one-sided, and despite his marriage, he fails to break away from what Brinkmeyer describes as his isolated consciousness.

Braggioni's passion for Laura is another instance of his one-sided emotional self-indulgence also based on his complete neglect and ignorance of the other party's, Laura's, feeling about the situation. He can manipulate her actions to suit his willfulness and schemes regardless of what is in her mind. Like Braggioni's wife, Laura is another main outlet of his emotional needs as well as the object of his sexual desire. Although she does not actually sleep with him while the narration takes place, like his wife, she is quite convenient for him. She sits quite docilely, at least as she appears to him, and lets him accost and make fun of her without showing him any sign of protest no matter how rudely he acts, just as his wife shows him no sign of reproach or demand. Obeying his request, she helps him prepare his pistols and sits with the shells that keep slipping through the oil-dipped cleaning cloth, while he unfastens his ammunition belt and spreads it laden on her knees. The scene has been interpreted as full of obvious phallic imagery and as Laura's symbolic surrender to Braggioni's sexual aggression. In this particular scene, he insults Laura, saying that he finds it quite odd that she appears to be rather involved in the revolution though she does not seem to be in love with anyone in it:

> "Are you not in love with someone?" "No," says Laura. "And no one is in love with you?" "No." "Then it is your own fault. No woman need go begging. Why, what is the matter with you? The legless beggar woman in the Alameda has a perfectly faithful lover. Did you know that?" (*Flowering Judas* 156)

We see here that one of Braggioni's ideas of women is that they are not capable of any significant mental concept other than matters relating to procreation. In his view, they are incapable and not worthy of ideas such as revolution. He does not think that women are perceptive and capable of analyzing and planning situations. That is why he finds them handy and safe to use and to expose his emotions and undisguised thoughts to. He does not see that they also have feelings and ideas and are potentially capable of perceiving his faults and opposing him if they intend to. Because he is completely blind to Laura's real feelings and thoughts, he keeps pouring out to her quite guilelessly whatever he now really thinks of the revolution and of the men still working and suffering for it. We see from what he tells her and from what she thinks of him that his view of the revolution is now quite corrupt. He now means to use the revolution to make a profit for himself; he thinks that the men involved in it are all stupid and that he can manipulate and use them easily. If any of them ever finds out from Laura what he now really thinks, things could possibly turn out not as safe for him as he believes, but he feels Laura is quite harmless, because her actions are mostly entirely passive. If she ever tries to express her clear opinion or to inquire, it becomes unpleasant for him and he immediately leaves, just as he leaves right away whenever his wife appears to criticize his wantonness with women. Toward the closing of the story when Laura starts to mention the horror of Eugenio's death, he is not in a good mood anymore and departs. If Laura ever steps a bit further than slightly showing her doubt of the situation, which is the furthest she now dares to go, and protests to him, it will be very dangerous for her. This means that the part of her from which he usually manages to avert his thoughts is incompatible with what he wants. The same is true with what is really in the minds of his wife and the men working for him for the cause. Therefore Braggioni's consciousness never merges with those of others because he always refuses to face what is in the minds of others: their fears, despair, fatigue, doubts, and frustration.

On Laura's part, yielding to and living within the corrupted system Braggioni has established, however unwilling she may be, destines her to isolation, too. Although Laura is passive and thus appears to be a victim of Braggioni's manipulation and the situation, her passivity has been interpreted by critics as her intentional strategy to preserve her own self and well-being. Such an interpretation regards her as responsible for being similar to Braggioni. By having chosen to be passive, even by camouflaging and sacrificing her genuine intentions, Laura has completely lost emotional and mental strength and energy. It is very hard for her to break away from the apathy she has fallen into because she feels that the mode by which she now earns a living is, in a sense, comfortable. She believes that the way of life that she has established for herself is effective for mere survival and for ensuring material comfort. She also believes that the firm wall that she has built up against any open emotion, passion, and relationships with others protects her from emotional troubles as well. In any kind of contact she has with others, she refuses to open herself and to let her emotions be moved by relationships. Her seemingly docile and submissive attitude towards Braggioni is only superficial and comes from her sheer calculation to retain material merits, while inside she seethes with resentment and protest. She refuses to expose herself to passion when other men approach her, because she wants to avoid any intimate relationship with anybody. Even with the children she teaches at school she puts up her guard against intimacy and condescends to their open playfulness and friendliness towards her. She thinks that her guard is flawless, gives her "strength," and keeps her "in safety": "her negation of all external events as they occur is a sign that she is gradually perfecting herself in the stoicism she strives to cultivate against that disaster she fears" (151). She believes that "one monotonous word," "No. No. No" is her sole means of protecting herself: "She draws her strength from this one holy talismanic word which does not suffer her to be led into evil. Denying everything, she may walk anywhere in safety" (151). However, the life of complete and immaculate negation is not as perfect as she wants to believe it to be and is not free of fatal drawbacks, especially emotional ones. Despite her conviction that the wall of negation is without any weakness, instead, it leaves her most weak inside. That is, it leads her to the weakness of confusion.

She faces the worst case of confusion at the end of the story when she tries to fall asleep, the most perfect form of negation. "Numbers tick in her brain like little clocks, soundless doors close of themselves around her." She tells herself, "If you would sleep, you must not remember anything." However, the ticking continues to disturb her terribly: "1-2-3-4-5—it is monstrous to confuse love with revolution, night with day, life with death–ah, Eugenio!" (159). In this scene, the choice Laura has made to sacrifice and exchange humane elements with material values finally affects her life by robbing her of sound sleep and wildly shakes her guard to remain absolutely uninfluenced and undisturbed. In trying to fall asleep, her subconscious awareness begins to emerge and she can no longer keep up her guard. Instead of being lulled to the sweetness of undisturbed sleep, she suddenly realizes that as the result of having forsaken humane elements in her life she is now left with only the elements of the machine world as is symbolized by the wild mechanical ticking of numbers. The materialistic and mechanical elements that Braggioni and the revolution represent as opposed to humane, compassionate elements, are now threatening Laura in the form of inhumane ticking sounds. She finally becomes conscious of the monstrosity of what she has sacrificed, especially of the high cost of not having distinguished love and revolution, life and death. In the middle of this realization, she suddenly perceives what she has caused in the life of one of the men for whom she has carried things to a prison, Eugenio, and her consciousness begins to merge with his. This is the only moment in the whole story at which Laura ever perceives the longings and fears of another individual. Also the last paragraph in the story is the only part in which Laura finally overcomes her fears. For the first time she pays attention to the words of another person without too much hesitation: "Without a word, without fear she rose and reached for Eugenio's hand" (159). Even after Eugenio has taken her some way through a strange and eerie landscape, she is still not so intimidated: "Where are you taking me, she asked in wonder but without fear" (160). However, it happens only in her dream, and not in reality. At the end of the dream, she goes back to the state in which she has always been when she is awake, again utters that "holy talismanic word," "No" (151), and breaks away from the dream and tries to deny it, being left to be afraid to fall asleep again. In departing her dream, she escapes from the desolate landscape Eugenio tries to invite her to and settles again into her previous isolated self.

Dreaming and being close to death bring up the subconsciousness and suppressed emotion and passion of another female protagonist of Porter's, in "The Jilting of Granny Weatherall." Ellen Weatherall was denied the fulfillment of her passion in her youth in an unexpected and blunt way by being "jilted" on the day of the wedding when she was twenty years old. The incident causes her the rest of her life to exert herself by all means not to remember the day and the man. In trying to do so, she concentrates on work and chores at her household. Her drive to work hard is accelerated by her strong determination and wish to completely forget the incident and the man and not to be let down by it. The extent of her capability and devotion to work is in proportion to her great need to emotionally do away with the traumatic memory of the day. She has been quite successful in shoving it away from her everyday life and her consciousness. In fact after she passes her adolescence the circumstances of her life have been so difficult in many ways that she has had no other choice but to work to the limit to merely survive. Had it not been for her exceeding strength and capability, she and her family would not have been able to make it through. Just as in many other stories by Porter about a strong matriarch who sustains a whole family, Granny Weatherall is the central figure in her household among weaker children and servants. Other members of the family could afford to be dependent on her and remain weaker than she is, while she felt that she had no alternative but to get over her misery, grow strong and manage severe difficulties.[5]

Despite the trials she had to face, she remembers rather fondly the hard days during which she always had company, and feels content and proud about her family life and her own exertions. Caring for family and others has enabled her not to remember that she was deserted by a person she loved and she hardly needed to think about and look into the state of isolation the person caused her to be in. For instance, she affectionately recollects the struggles of having raised her own children: "Little things, little things! They had been so sweet when they were little" (*Flowering Judas* 126). It is narrated that she even "wished the old days were back again with the children young and everything to be done over. It had been a hard pull, but not too much for her" (126-27). Instead of harping on the betrayal by George, she has always cared much and worked for others both in her own household and in the community at their most trying times. "Riding country roads in the winter when women had babies was another thing: sitting up nights with sick horses and sick negroes and sick children and hardly ever losing one" (83). After she becomes delirious from sickness, and even at the moment of her death, she keeps caring and thinks of the needs of others. For others she pleads,

> Oh, my dear Lord, do wait a minute. I meant to do something about the Forty Acres, Jimmy doesn't need it and Lydia will later on, with that worthless husband of hers. I meant to finish the altar cloth and send six bottles of wine to Sister Borgia for her dyspepsia. I want to send six bottles of wine to Sister Borgia, Father Connolly, now don't let me forget. (135)

However, being strong and proud by nature, she has never entreated others to help her overcome her major loss, although on her part she did everything possible to survive it by working hard all through her life for sixty years. Part of the reason she did not lean on others in her attempt to do away with the unhappy memory has been because being jilted by George has hurt her innermost self and the wound inflicted on that part of her self could not be shared with others. She felt that words and deeds of others could not heal it, nor did she want to unfold her inmost wound to others. The states of isolation she goes through in her life between twenty and eighty have caused her to realize that some ultimate states of isolation are inevitable in life and that one cannot annihilate them even if one strives to. For sixty years she has splendidly managed not to be halted by three major experiences of desertion by or separation from the ones she loved. At first George left her. Then John, the person she married, dies early, and her favorite daughter, Hapsy, dies in childbirth.

All three of these experiences begin to come to her delirious mind when she is finally on the threshold of dying. Only the approach of death could make the headstrong woman be stopped by these memories. Finally, Granny Weatherall is departing the present life for eternal rest, and for the first time drops her constant and resolute exertions not to be halted by them. She begins to talk to the three from whom she has been separated against her wishes and to draw conclusions about what she finally thinks of them and her relation with and separation from them. With John she feels that he would understand her completely for what she has managed and how and why she has changed, while with George her ultimate conclusion is that she will never forgive him. She talks to Hapsy and tells her that she finally wants to join her.

In her communion with the deceased and the loved and her reminiscence of the person who inflicted the deepest wound when she was twenty years old, Ellen Weatherall departs the world of the living where consciousness dominates. She begins to enter the realm of subconsciousness and ultimate isolation, that is, isolation from living people and from the rational elements of the daily world of consciousness. As she does so, the unbridgeable cleavage and unbreakable wall begin to build up between her and living people who are aware of and value only the rational elements belonging to the realm of consciousness. The thoughts that come to her as she enters her final state are irrational and disorderly from the viewpoint of someone living in daily life. The living family and people who surround her at her deathbed cannot understand them. On her part, she cannot control the thoughts in a way she has always managed to have control over the rows of bottles of ingredients in her house and orderly rows of crops in the field, and over the severities she has conquered. In the delirious condition she is now in she finally faces the state of her psychology that she has long suppressed to physically survive. Finally she cannot exert control over the effect of the passion she had for George in her youth, over the destructive force it has had on her once it was unrequited, and over the state of isolation the thwarted passion has placed her in.

In "The Jilting of Granny Weatherall" we observe prototypical, forceful examples of the relation between passion and isolation. Being denied her passion condemns Ellen to the most extreme form of isolation for her, becomes representative of existential isolation, and causes her to face the ultimate abyss. Porter depicts the immeasurable chasm that Ellen begins to have glimpses of on her deathbed through the imagery of darkness and smothering smoke. The imagery portrays how an ultimate isolation bears pressure on the existence of an individual as well as how deep it is. The darkness of damnation is contrasted with the scene of daylight and an open field.[6]

> Such a fresh breeze blowing and such a green day with no threats in it. . . .
> There was the day, the day, but a whirl of dark smoke rose and covered it, crept
> up and over into the bright field where everything was planted so carefully in
> orderly rows. That was hell, she knew hell when she saw it. For sixty years she
> had prayed against remembering him and against losing her soul in the deep pit
> of hell, and now the two things were mingled in one and the thought of him
> was a smoky cloud from hell that moved and crept in her head. (128-29)

What the loss has led her to turns out to be more than she can exert control over. Ellen cannot help realize that "there was something else" besides what she has strived and believed to have won back against what she had lost in being jilted, despite all she has done. "Oh, no, oh, God, no, there was something else. . . . Her breath crowded down under her ribs and grew into a monstrous frightening shape with cutting edges; it bored up into her head, and the agony was unbelievable" (131).

Although Ellen Weatherall finds the darkness of the isolation unbearably painful and suffocating, however, we also strikingly observe in "The Jilting of Granny Weatherall" that the desire of the protagonist to retreat finally into the darkness and solitude characterizes the state of her isolation. This is especially true in the way she faces her own psychology concerning the experience of having been jilted. For instance, earlier in the story, she wants, by any means, to conceal from her offspring and anybody what she went through in her youth and its effect on her. She wants to destroy all the correspondence between herself and George and John so as not to let them find out her innermost experience, that is, "how silly she had been once" (124). At a more profound level, immediately after she begins to see and is tormented by the infernal vision of "the deep pit of hell" and "a smoky cloud from hell," she also begins to want to escape from the illumination of the world of light and day (128-29).

> Her eyelids wavered and let in streamers of blue-gray light like tissue paper
> over her eyes. She must get up and pull the shades down or she'd never sleep.
> She was in bed again and the shades were not down. How could that happen?
> Better turn over, hide from the light, sleeping in the light gave you nightmares.
> (129)

Her desire to withdraw into darkness in this part of the story symbolizes her final desire to do away with the rational arguments of the daily world. Although she quickly attempts to cast away "a whirl of dark smoke" by telling herself that only her "vanity" has been "wounded" in her being jilted and to argue that she should be able to stand it, at the very last moment, she cannot bear such rationalization anymore (128-29). It puts her into "nightmares" rather than relieves her (129).

When she is even closer to death toward the end of the story, another vision of the imagery of light appears to her: "Light flashed on her closed eyelids, and a deep roaring shook her" (135). The light is from the lightning in an envisioned thunderstorm. It symbolizes the abrupt manner in which death visits and astounds her. In the middle of her astonishment at how massive, violent, and sudden death is, as was the blow of being jilted in her youth, Ellen Weatherall suddenly perceives "a tiny point" "of light" (136). It is very small and contrasts with the enormous size of the nightmarish vision the bold daylight has given her and of the terror of the lightning as well as of the monstrous darkness that attacks and enfolds her several times in the story. It is tiny and weak compared with the greater shadow that is about to swallow it. At this point Ellen grows "watchful," although she is also "amazed." Growing vigilant, she spots the light in the very "center of her brain," "staring at the point" (136). She clearly recognizes that the light there is "herself" (136). The last line of the story describes the way Ellen Weatherall finally dies: "She stretched herself with a deep breath and blew out the light" (136). She finally accepts her end and blows out the light of her life and self in an act of her own. The line sums up how she reaches self-recognition and self-assertion in the middle of ultimate isolation, the incurred memory of the thwarted passion and the final process of dying. Her assertion is that the significance and the meaning of her existence will not be annihilated by the blunt manner in which another person treated her in the past. Although it may be small and dwindle, it is as clear as a point of light, and her act to terminally extinguish it signifies the acceptance on her part. The final confirmation of her self, in the form of the vision of a tiny point of light in the center of her brain, enables her to finally accept the core of herself. In isolation from which she will never return, she allows herself to accept the unhealed sorrow of the failure of her passion. She could do this only in the state of ultimate isolation. Acceptance of herself within final isolation subsequently leads her to the acquiescence to the fact of death.

Notes

1. Gretlund in his discussion on Welty and Chekhov points out that in Welty's stories the main focus is on character development rather than on plot and actions. "The careful arrangement of selected details and the emphasis on the individual life and place often cause the overall plot development to be vague in both writers. They tend to rate character development above the organization of the action. No matter how dramatic an event, it still seems to occur by chance. . . . There is no attempt to avoid the dramatic incident; but the drama and the violence are never in the stories to entertain. The focus

remains squarely on the growth of the individual characters, and the dramatic events serve to tell us about them" (325).

2. Welty comments on "At the Landing" in *Conversations with Eudora Welty*, and frankly states that it is not perfect as a story. She adds that she was most preoccupied with capturing the mood of the river-town rather than other elements of the story while writing it, admitting that such a particular emphasis may have distorted other makings of the story.

3. Critics have taken the schoolgirl of "A Memory" as an artist figure. Especially her gesture of framing a rectangular perspective with fingers has been pointed to as an act of an artist. (Examples: Cheryll Burgess 135, Ruth M. Vande Kieft 45-47).

4. Porter condensed much of the revolting aspects that she had witnessed while she was involved in revolution in Mexico into the one character of Braggioni in "Flowering Judas" as she mentions in one of the interviews compiled in *Katherine Anne Porter: Conversations* (123).

5. There are two critical interpretations of her resolution to work hard so as not to be defeated by the emotional effect of having been jilted. According to many critics, her determination to overcome the emotional effect of having been jilted causes her to suppress her emotion. Thus her life wastes into a bitterness engendered by an unreleased emotion. Many of them categorize "The Jilting of Granny Weatherall" among Porter's fictional works whose themes are failure and wasted life. Among such criticisms are "Negatives of Hope: A Reading of Katherine Anne Porter" by Joseph Wiesenfarth, and the analysis by Vanashree in the section, "Feminine Subterfuge," in *Feminine Consciousness in Katherine Anne Porter's Fiction*. Others commend her strength and determination. Among them Tanner clearly acclaims Ellen Weatherall's accomplishment and her strong will, although he also recognizes the theme of the wasted life.

6. Darlene Harbour Unrue treats the image of light and darkness in detail in *Truth and Vision in Katherine Anne Porter's Fiction*. Unrue interprets light in "The Jilting of Granny Weatherall" as symbolizing the truth and order that Granny seeks so as to save herself from her fear of darkness and disruptive memory that are in turn represented by the image of dark fog or smoke (Unrue 99-101).

Chapter 3

Family and Isolation

In her article, "Family in Eudora Welty's Fiction," Sara McAlpin BVM points out that one of the clearly noticeable characteristics of American southern writers is their emphasis on family, although she admits that the labeling, "southern," is a complex notion. She observes that Welty is one of the most important writers from the American South who repeatedly and extensively deals with the complex nature of the family (299). Welty frequently treats in her stories the intricate layers of sympathy and antipathy within families. As Welty, Porter, and other southern writers portray in their works, a family always bears problematic elements for each of its members, although the unit is one of the most basic collective groups in human society, and no one escapes the influence of its bond. Family bonds do not always alleviate the state of isolation of an individual, but problems in families can aggravate the state of isolation. The trials within a family can destroy an individual member in many cases once problems are out of control. On the other hand, people attempt to survive and cope with adversities and vicissitudes occurring within and falling upon families. Often, complex problems within a family interact inseparably with the culture containing it.

"Flowers for Marjorie" by Welty exhibits a severe form of separation within a marital relationship. In the course of the story, Howard's separation from his pregnant wife reaches the extreme when he hates her and murders her, despite their seeming closeness to each other. They live together and Marjorie is expecting their baby in three months. The author effectively describes their being in the same room on the day he murders her to paradoxically accentuate their severe psychological isolation from each other. Howard now hates the way Marjorie's attention seems to him to be exclusively directed to the life inside her and not to anything else. Even when they are together in the same small room, his wife seems so unattainable and he feels utterly isolated. When Marjorie al-

ludes to the subject of Howard's unemployment, he suddenly starts and instinc-
tively puts distance between them. The physical distance between them in the
scene is symbolic of the psychological discrepancy between them. It grows more
and more irrecoverable as they talk. When Howard's hostility against Marjorie
grows more and more keen, he literally pushes himself to the wall and is driven
into a corner. He "moved even further back until he stood against the wall, as far
as possible away from Marjorie, as though she were faithless and strange, allied
to the other forces" (198). When the tension he feels toward her is in its extreme
shortly before he stabs her, the distance between them is completed: "Away at
his distance, backed against the wall, he regarded her world . . . grown forever
apart" (199).

The grave irony that Welty successfully captures in "Flowers for Marjorie"
is that all the supposedly positive elements in Marjorie, the wife and expectant
mother, serve to enlarge the discrepancy between Marjorie and Howard instead
of joining the two. The contrast between Howard and Marjorie at the time of the
narration is emphasized as the cause of the rift between them. On one hand, being unemployed without a prospect of being employed seriously affects Howard's emotional condition. He suffers from a grim sense of failure, loss, sterility
and despair. On the other hand, expecting a baby before long, Marjorie beams in
fullness, happiness and fertility. Both Howard and Marjorie fail to see what
might be his or her own part in the situation of the other spouse. Possibly they
have no other choice except to reproach each other. They never attempt to take
any part in what happens to the other. Concerning Howard's unemployment,
Marjorie only admonishes him for staying unemployed. In her view she can do
nothing about it except to hope that he will keep trying and that he will get a job
before long. This thought is intensified by her conviction that she is doing her
own part perfectly in being soundly pregnant. Although Howard is the father of
the expected baby, he is not able to appreciate her pregnancy. Being in despair,
he has lost any sense of hope and cannot appreciate anything wholesome and
bright. Consequently Marjorie's pregnancy and the way she glows in hope intensify Howard's despair instead of solacing him in any way.

Marjorie is the epitome of fullness, hope, beauty, and softness, but her assets become a smothering pressure and a menace for Howard. He reacts nerv-
ously to the presence and the radiance of anything wholesome and beautiful. His
reaction to them is violent and destructive. He either convulsively backs away
from them, or impulsively destroys them. His murder of Marjorie is foreshad-
owed by his enigmatic repulsion and sudden destruction of a pansy. The bright-
ness of the flower represents the happy radiance of Marjorie as she proudly
waves it in front of him. The narration of how only one small flower becomes a
threat to him just because it is bright and is brought in by Marjorie is illustrative.
"It was bright yellow. She only found it, Howard thought, but he winced inwardly, as though she had displayed some power of the spirit. He simply had to
sit and stare at her, his hands drawn back into his pockets" (194). When Howard
averts his eyes from the fullness of Marjorie, he catches the sight of the pansy
again, and is startled by it.

There it shone, a wide-open yellow flower with dark red veins and edges. Against the sky-blue of Marjorie's old coat it began in Howard's anxious sight to lose its identity of flower-size and assume the gradual and large curves of a mountain on the horizon of a desert, the veins becoming crevasses, the delicate edges the giant worn lips of a sleeping crater. His heart jumped to his mouth. (195)

Howard's hallucination that he destroys it at this moment when his loathing of it culminates is parallel to his psychological state when he stabs Marjorie later. Another parallel between Howard's hallucination and his murder of Marjorie is that Marjorie remains completely undisturbed and calm in both of the scenes. While Howard is having this strange and violent vision about the pansy, Marjorie remains completely calm. Marjorie's reaction to Howard's frenzy is always perfectly tranquil. Even when he holds a butcher knife toward her, she still does not see that he is desperate to the point of insanity. She is not alarmed at all and makes only a mild, murmuring inquiry "in a patient, lullaby-like voice," as she always has had (199). Her pacifying tone and attitude, however, complete the tension between her and Howard instead of alleviating it.

Just as the vision of the pansy grows in Howard's thoughts, Marjorie and her splendid ease grow out of proportion, and suffocate and menace him. After a fruitless day looking for a job, the thought of her is an unwelcome assault on him that drains his spirit.

Always now like something he had put off, the thought of her was like a wave that hit him when he was tired, rising impossibly out of stagnancy and deprecation while he sat in the park, towering over his head, pounding, falling, going back and leaving nothing behind it. (193)

When they talk about the baby and a job, the softer Marjorie's body, voice, and demeanor become, the more Howard is pressed and driven to despair. The subjects of the baby and a job are now the central concerns of their family life, but Howard hates to think about them and wants to completely avoid talking about them, while Marjorie emphasizes them at every turn. She does not discern Howard's despair and insanity, and wants to be together with him and to discuss the subjects. She is all gentleness and warmth, but Howard feels suffocated in the sweet scent of her skin and her voluptuous thighs. When he lays his face on her breast and she gently lays her hand on him while holding him, he thinks inwardly, "Why, this is not possible!" (197). He feels "new desperation" rising in him every second "in the time-marked softness and the pulse of her sheltering body" (197).

To Howard, Marjorie and her pregnancy represent the regularity of the real world, as is symbolized by his detestation and destruction of a clock. The state of unemployment makes him feel that he is placed outside the frame of the natural, normal world. As Diana R. Pingatore restates Peter Schmidt's analysis of the story, Howard fears the natural and organic order.[1] Marjorie's beauty, her soft body, her pregnancy and contentment as well as the organic beauty of the pansy and the regularity of the ticking of a clock are all horrifying representations of the natural order for Howard. After he destroys them all, he goes out of the house into the city. However, his departure for the excursion does not mark the beginning of the real experiences that he might have recovered by getting rid of Marjorie.[2] To the contrary, Marjorie's murder completes his withdrawal from reality into the unreal, as he goes out into the streets. Howard has always had a strong inclination to shut his eyes and withdraw from reality. By killing Marjorie, Howard tentatively manages to shut reality away completely. Now he does not have to see the organic growth inside her anymore, and nobody will insistently question him about the search for a job. What is left for him after Marjorie and the life inside her cease to exist are things that let him escape from reality. Going out of the house into the streets, he walks into an unreal, comic, and purposeless world. He passes by shops that sell and display toys, funny things used for pranks, and other odd miscellanies. In one of the shops, for a moment he is fascinated by a small paperweight with a little, bright scene inside. He wishes to be there in the world inside the small glass. For the first time in the story, Howard smiles. "It made him smile: it was like everything made small and illuminated and flowering, not too big now" (202). His playful wish in the scene is characteristic of his inclination to stay within the compact neatness of the unreal world. He finds temporary relief in seeing the contained scene. He feels he can handle miniature things. They will not threaten him. However, by this point in the story, it is only an irrational, pathetic, comic relief, because Howard's world has already been subverted by his murder of Marjorie.

Another story by Welty, "A Curtain of Green," also treats a predicament that destroys the matrimonial life of a couple. Like "Flowering Judas" and "The Jilting of Granny Weatherall" by Porter and "Flowers for Marjorie" by Welty, it explores how the theme of isolation closely intertwines with the theme of death and violence. "A Curtain of Green" presents the case of isolation of a young widow, Mrs. Larkin, whose husband died in an arbitrary accident one year before the narration begins. One day a chinaberry tree in front of their house unexpectedly fell and crushed his car. Mrs. Larkin witnessed the accident while she waited on the porch to see him come home. As noted by critics, readers find similarity between the nature of love and isolation of Mrs. Larkin and those of a schoolgirl, "I," in "Memory" discussed in the previous chapter. Both in "A Curtain of Green" and "Memory" the female protagonists suffer from a realization that their love for the ones they love cannot necessarily protect them. In "Memory" the schoolgirl has a premonition about the danger that might befall the boy she loves and is initiated into the experience of isolation. In "A Curtain of Green" Mrs. Larkin did not anticipate such a hazard. When she softly uttered "her protective words," "You can't be hurt," she did not imagine that the falling of the tree would actually kill her husband (214). But it did.

After his death, she spends her time every day in her garden, fiercely battling with its "tangled," "over-abundant," and "confusing" growth (210). Her manner is described as "over-vigorous, disreputable, and heedless" (210). She is completely negligent of her appearance as she ceaselessly works in a man's overalls that make her look even more strange. The heat of the sun and the heavy rain that summer never stop her.

Welty sets the heedless, unkempt, enigmatic figure of Mrs. Larkin in sharp contrast with the life of her neighbors in the town of Larkin's Hill. Although their lives are in the background of the narration and none of their indivi-dual names and actual comments are directly introduced, the difference between them and Mrs. Larkin provides a significant clue for the understanding of the puzzle of Mrs. Larkin's ferocious activity in the garden. Although the narration does not describe the life and personality of Mrs. Larkin prior to the death of her husband, readers infer that his death changed her situation and status in the community. Before his death, Mrs. Larkin was presumably an honored member of the community. The town, Larkin's Hill was named after Mr. Larkin's father (212). After his death, Mrs. Larkin does not fit into the community anymore, which aggravates the state of her isolation caused by the death of Mr. Larkin.

Among critical interpretations of "A Curtain of Green," the discussion by Charlotte C. Hadella gives an extensive commentary on the meaning of the con-trast between Mrs. Larkin and the women in the neighborhood. In the chapter "Eudora Welty's Gardens: Lonely Ladies and Landscapes," in her dissertation, *Women in Gardens in American Short Fiction*, Hadella commends the character of Mrs. Larkin after her husband's death for its vitality and passion, as is shown in her forceful working and her inclination to keep her garden wild and profuse rather than taming and trimming it, although she acknowledges that the loneli-ness of Mrs. Larkin is not self-imposed. Contrasting Mrs. Larkin and other women in the community, Hadella argues that the life of the women in the community is barren and void of meaningful activities. As Hadella aptly points out, while Mrs. Larkin merges with nature, her female neighbors shut it out. At the beginning of the story, the women in town wait for rain in a passive manner that characterizes their genteel indoor life and their lack of vitality. As for the purpose of gardens, they think that one aims at "an effect of restfulness" and "harmony," and would "elect in their club as to what constituted an appropriate vista" of gardens (212). There are also sets of socially acceptable norms such as sending flowers from one's garden when neighbors are sick or pass away. Mrs. Larkin and her garden entirely deviate from the ideas and codes of the commu-nity.

The author intersperses the comments of the neighbors, as if they whisper behind Mrs. Larkin in the background, to illustrate how Mrs. Larkin and her garden are a complete enigma to them, and how they are totally incapable of sympathizing with the psychology that drives her to act in her garden in the way she does. They only think that her garden is not presentable, without realizing the connection between its confusing over-growth and her desperation. How-ever, Welty clearly suggests its meaning: "To a certain extent, she seemed not to seek for order, but to allow an overflowing, as if she consciously ventured for-ever a little farther, a little deeper, into her life in the garden" (211). Mrs. Larkin is engrossed and immersed in the exploration for the fundamental meaning of life, and delves unhesitatingly into the core of the mystery of life. Although the isolation into which she has been placed by the death of Mr. Larkin is not what she wanted, to have been exposed to the severe fate and to face the unfathomable isolation have awakened her to seek the "farther," "deeper" meaning (211). Unlike Mrs. Larkin, her neighbors remain in an insipid mode of life as they remain blind to the turbulence, unpredictable turns, hardships, perplexities, and meanings of life. They shut their eyes from them. They are content to stay in a protected and safe, but uninteresting, mode of life as they glance rather condescendingly at the small, striving figure of Mrs. Larkin and her garden "from their upstairs windows" (212). They regard Mrs. Larkin and her garden as something totally alien and unrelated to their own lives. When they show any interest, at best they are mildly inquisitive, and soon completely forget her to go back to their daily lives to tend to what they think is more important than observing something strange and useless. Society has molded their minds to be insipid and empty to the extent that it does not occur to them anymore that any senseless, chance misfortune could visit them, too, at any time.

In view of the attitudes and notions of the women in the neighborhood, one can expect and understand Mrs. Larkin's reaction to the visitors in the initial period of mourning. "But she had not appreciated it, they said to one another" (212). Mrs. Larkin understandably would not have, because the sympathies of the women in the community would not have been genuine. Readers can picture the isolated figure of Mrs. Larkin as she receives the callers. At best, the calls are social formalities. Mrs. Larkin would have appreciated even less those who stopped by out of inquisitiveness to see what had befallen the once honored family. The women in the community are incapable of sensing the despair and isolation of Mrs. Larkin.

Although one may assess the significance and value of Mrs. Larkin's endeavor and criticize the bland life of the other women in the community, Mrs. Larkin's gain is not brought to her without struggle and pain. Welty stresses the severe agony of Mrs. Larkin as well as her energetic strivings. On the particular day when the narration takes place, Mrs. Larkin is in the most despondent state of mind. Welty always matches the psychological condition of the protagonist and the condition of the weather that surrounds her in "A Curtain of Green" so as to symbolically illustrate through natural imagery how she struggles and copes with isolation. On the day described in the story, from the afternoon on, the tension in Mrs. Larkin rises, as the day remains hot without the regular afternoon rain to relieve the heat. After her continuous work in the garden, her eyes look strained and dejected, and her mouth is tightly shut. In the unmitigated heat of the day, the tragic recollection of the accident that killed Mr. Larkin repeats itself in her mind without warning, "as if a curtain had been jerked quite unceremoniously away from a little scene" (109). After the tormenting details have been repeated in her mind against her wish not to remember them, her psychological strain and isolation are heightened to the limit. The scorching weather intensifies them. Everything stops in that moment as if to accentuate her uneasiness.

Presently she became aware that hers was the only motion to continue in the whole slackened place. There was no wind at all now. The cries of the birds had hushed. The sun seemed clamped to the side of the sky. Everything had stopped once again, the stillness had mesmerized the stems of the plants, and all the leaves went suddenly into thickness. The shadow of the pear tree in the center of the garden lay callous on the ground. Across the yard, Jamey knelt, motionless. (214)

When she suddenly realizes that her angry voice does not carry in the thick garden to awaken the hired boy from his stupor to move and work in the garden again, she becomes horrified, suddenly being more keenly and acutely aware of her isolation than ever.

She felt all at once terrified, as though her loneliness had been pointed out by some outside force whose fingers parted the hedge. She drew her hand for an instant to her breast. An obscure fluttering there frightened her, as though the force babbled to her. The bird that flies within your heart could not divide this cloudy air . . . (215)

She grows even more high-strung when she looks at the soft, innocent face of Jamey, whose mind wanders in some reverie as he stops working and does not move. Then suddenly and hopelessly, she is seized by intense despair rising within her. She becomes infuriated about the unreasonableness of the death of her spouse and of the way it has bluntly thrown her into her present isolation. She questions intently: "Was it not possible to compensate? to punish? to protest?" (217). In her query and protest that are not answered, she raises her hoe behind and above the unmoving head of Jamey.

However, right at the moment when Mrs. Larkin is about to strike Jamey, the rain finally begins to fall, and its soothing effect relieves her tension and prevents her from committing murder. The rain soothes and heals her without answering. Welty concludes the story to affirm the suffering, severe tension, and lonely psychological struggles of Mrs. Larkin without attempting to give an answer to the protest of Mrs. Larkin. The author lets Mrs. Larkin be fully exposed to and soaked in the symbolical benefit of the rain and nature. Mrs. Larkin alone among all the women in the town of Larkin's Hill has opened herself to and has probed deep enough into nature to be able to appreciate its merits. She falls among the flowers and remains totally submerged among them and the falling rain. She lies there in complete submission, although the submission is no solution. She thinks of the rain "senselessly," while turning her eyes "without understanding at the sky" (111). She thinks that she will now finally rest, while contemplating that "against that which was inexhaustible, there was no defense" (218). She becomes like "a sleeper" who moves only slightly (214). Her figure becomes "shapeless" and "passive," her face, "unknowing" (219).

Out of her struggles against and within her isolation, Mrs. Larkin has attained the state of acquiescence. She alone is immersed in nature and the rain at the end of the story. The beauty and the purifying, enlivening effect of the rain are revealed to her alone, who has taken a daring step of seeking "a little farther, a little deeper, into her life in the garden" (211).

> In the light from the rain, different from sunlight, everything appeared to gleam unreflecting from within itself in its quiet arcade of identity. The green of the small zinnia shoots was very pure, almost burning. One by one, as the rain reached them, all the individual little plants shone out, and then the branching vines. The pear tree gave a soft rushing noise, like the wings of a bird alighting. (217)

Finally, Welty lets Mrs. Larkin be united with and be tenderly immersed into nature.

Many of Porter's short stories also treat the failure of the relationships within a family. "María Concepción," "Rope," "The Cracked Looking-Glass," "That Tree," and "A Day's Work," first published in this order, all depict rifts within marital relationships. "María Concepción," written and published at the earliest date among these stories, deals with the darkest and the most violent form of a failed relationship between spouses of all these five short stories. As in the two stories by Welty discussed in this chapter, "Flowers for Marjorie" and "A Curtain of Green," it involves violence and death. Like the male protagonist, Howard, in "Flowers for Marjorie," the female protagonist commits murder in "María Concepción." María Concepción kills María Rosa, the mistress of her husband, Juan Villegas. The story involves another death, the death of the baby born to María Concepción and Juan four days after it is born. This happens after Juan and María Rosa run away to join a war. Readers of Porter's stories discern clear similarities between "María Concepción" and "The Jilting of Granny Weatherall" in that the plot of both includes betrayal and desertion of a woman by a man and the death of a child. Both of the female protagonists, María Concepción and Ellen Weatherall, are strong-willed women and both stand up to adversities, the betrayal by a man and the loss of a child, and function well. However, both continue to brood and harbor a deep and dark grudge against betrayal. Pride is a major part of the dispositions of both of them, and it makes it entirely impossible for them to control their rage.

Like Howard in "Flowers for Marjorie" by Welty, María Concepción commits murder out of desperation and a grim sense of isolation. Although she is admirably capable of managing to make a living after Juan elopes with María Rosa and the baby she gives birth to dies, inwardly she continues to boil with rage. On the surface, she might appear to be in complete control of her emotions. Critics commend her for her firm restraint from giving in to her emotion and sentimentality. However, does not Porter's eloquent, but efficient diction vividly depict the insurmountable intensity of her grief, fury, hatred, and uncontrollable drive for revenge, rather than her restraint? Although, later in retrospect, María Concepción feels content and thinks that the order of the world is restored after her murder of María Rosa and after other villagers and Juan protect her from being arrested, at the time she heads toward the hut of María Rosa, she is not in her senses. She does not even know what she intends to do. She does not realize until a moment later that she is set to kill María Rosa instead of going to market to sell fowls as usual.

> She fumbled and tangled the bits of cord in her haste, and set off across the plowed fields instead of taking the accustomed road. She ran with a crazy panic in her head, her stumbling legs. Now and then she would stop and look about her, trying to place herself, then go on a few steps, until she realized that she was not going toward the market. (*Flowering Judas* 20-21)

Finally at this moment she realizes what exactly troubles her and what she wants. She wants to kill María Rosa. She does not reach this decision through a rational sense of judgment. She certainly feels that the affair and the elopement of Juan and María Rosa are unjust acts beyond limit, but her judgment stems rather from her outrage and indescribable personal misery than from a detached, objective sense of justice.[3] The moment she recognizes the exact spot of her agony, for the first time she gives herself time to give in to grief. Her emotional pain is so severe that it begins to affect the condition of her body, and she begins to perspire heavily. However, she gives in to her emotion, while sitting alone without being seen by anybody. Her posture in the scene symbolizes the severity of her isolation. She is immobile, unseen, and speechless. "She sat down quietly under a sheltering thorny bush and gave herself over to her long devouring sorrow. . . . Drawing her rebozo over her head, she bowed her forehead on her up-drawn knees, and sat there in deadly silence and immobility" (21). She looks as if she were crying, but "no tears and no sound" come out (21). Unlike Mrs. Larkin in Welty's "A Curtain of Green" María Concepción fails to find a release from her hardened emotion. Her emotional pain is described as having formed "a tight dumb knot of suffering" (21). She feels that her whole being is "a dark confused memory" (21). When she finally stands up and starts to walk again, she realizes that she can no longer live with the suffering and fury that have not been vented. She will release them. However, the measure she finally takes to cope with her emotional crisis is the most destructive one. She will kill the mistress of her husband.

Although the story ends with the description of how serene and content María Concepción feels after she kills María Rosa and after she has been assured of the consent of the villagers and Juan to her act, the measure she has taken out of the most severe spite does not restore the union between her and Juan. Outwardly María Concepción gets rid of Juan's mistress and moreover has been found by the community to be just. However, the disappearance of María Rosa does not change Juan's nature, and he remains emotionally uninterested in María Concepción. He momentarily admires her and wants to repent when he hears from her of the murder and when she declares solemnly in darkness in "a tone so tender, so grave, so heavy with suffering" that for her "everything is settled now" between her and him (25). However, his feeling at that moment is from fear and shock, but not from genuine sympathy and remorse. Once he and

María Concepción, with the support of other villagers, manage to delude the officers attempting to investigate the murder and go back together to their hut as she carries the baby born to him and María Rosa, he only feels sullen and tired. He grudgingly muses that his merry days with María Rosa are over and that she has disappeared forever. He feels that now he only has dragging, boring days of "labor" ahead of him (33). To him, María Concepción now seems only "as unreal, as ghostly," and as insignificant "as the brushing of a leaf against his face" as they walk back (34). His momentary sense of adventure of saving her from being arrested entirely subsides. He has no idea why he exerted himself at all to save her, "and now he forgot her" (34). He feels bitter, sad, and hurt.

At the end of the story, María Concepción is portrayed as not paying much attention to how Juan feels and not questioning whether the strength of the relationship between herself and Juan has been truly redeemed. Although she fully tastes sweet contentment at the end of the story, apparently Juan does not. Whoever is the cause of the problem, María Concepción or Juan, the relationship between the two is not whole at the end. María Concepción's satisfaction at the end of the story is not so much as a wife as that of a member of the community and as a foster mother. It primarily rests on her having been approved and supported by other members of the community and on her having taken up raising the baby born between Juan and María Rosa, left after María Concepción's murder of her. María Concepción and Juan remain isolated from each other and fail to find satisfaction within their family life.

As critics observe, María Concepción is more preoccupied with the outward intactness of their marriage than in whether the relationship is genuine or not. As Judie James Hatchett observes, her obsessive concern with the appearance and the form of their marriage clouds her clear judgment of Juan's nature and conduct (Hatchett 110). She fails to objectively observe their relationship and the situation between her and Juan, and to detect the rift between them and the cause of the rift. The appearance and the form make María Concepción so content that she almost seems not to care much about the reality of the relationship. As Hatchett critically points out, what she considers most important and meaningful in her marriage is the fact that she and Juan got married in the church instead of behind it, which costs less and which is the common custom of most other Indian villagers (Hatchett 110). She is quite proud that they got married in a more expensive and auspicious way than fellow Indians (Hatchett 110). María Concepción never discerns that Juan never considers their marriage in the church as solemnly as she does. When he and María Rosa come back to the village after they get tired of marching in a war, Juan makes a comment on the marriage between him and María Concepción in the church. When his employer points out by that he is flippant "for a man who was married in the church," he says, "Look, my chief, to be married in the church is a great misfortune for a man. After that he is not himself any more" (17-18). The thought of her to whom he has been betrothed in the church gives him "a sinking inside," and he feels "as if something were lying heavy" on his stomach" (18). The only meaning he sees in his marriage to María in the church is very slight, as he casually continues to comment, "I would not harm María Concepción because I am married to her in the church" (18). Apparently his view of not hurting María Concepción is drastically divergent from hers. When Givens admonishes Juan, trying to relate to him the fierceness of María Concepción's anger, Juan says, "I do not beat her; never, never. We were always at peace" (18). Juan's basic notion is that, as long as he does not actually physically hurt her, he has not hurt her at all, so he does not hesitate to add that he will not give up indulging himself in his pleasure with María Rosa.

In her marital relationship with Juan, María Concepción is primarily concerned about the external actions that take place between them for meeting daily necessities. Juan's view of the marital relationship between them is similar to hers in that he also cares only about such external facts. María Concepción is proudly aware of her role as a wife, and faithfully and devotedly performs what she considers the duties of a wife. She cooks for Juan and carries food to him and his chief at their work, the excavation site. As Porter introduces her character in the beginning of the story, even when she is tired and may want to take some rest on the way there, she does not allow herself a minute, and places priority on the needs of her husband and his employer. She is wholly satisfied and proud of being that way. Just as she regards other Indians who marry in a less expensive and less ceremonious way beneath her, she despises Juan's chief, Givens, as "that diverting white man who had no woman of his own to cook for him, and moreover appeared not to feel any loss of dignity in preparing his own food" (10). Although Juan is not faithful to María Concepción, he sees her as a dutiful, dependable woman in managing daily necessities. He believes that is sufficient for him. He says of her, "I say to her, Come here, and she comes straight. I say, Go there, and she goes quickly" (18). Although this comment by Juan shows no respect for her and reveals that he does not see how she can emotionally seethe once she is hurt, in a sense, it accurately captures the resolute and reliable character of María, and the way both he and she value their relationship primarily in terms of the outward actions for managing daily life. As long as their daily living is managed, both of them continue to deceptively believe that the relationship between them is good, although the reason for Juan to believe so is quite different from why María believes so. She merely does not know, while Juan continues to indulge in womanizing, never stopping to think about what his conduct may cause in his marital relationship with María.

Notes

1. Pingatore mentions that Schmidt sums up the previous analyses of "Flowers for Marjorie." In Schmidt's interpretation, Marjorie represents natural and organic time and order, whereas Howard represents artificial and commercial time and order of urban scenes as is seen in his wandering among shops in the streets of the city in the second half of the story (Pingatore 128).

2. Naoko Fuwa Thornton believes that Howard restores reality and begins to act in it again, ironically after he commits the act that is the antithesis of his murder of Marjorie. That is, first, he blocks and stops real time and reality by murdering Marjorie, who repre-

Chapter 4

Feminine Independence and Isolation

Eudora Welty is quite famous for resisting the women's rights movement. As she states in "Must the Novelist Crusade?" in the second section, "On Writing," in *The Eye of the Story*, she does not believe that the role of literature and art is to "crusade" and to advocate and propagate causes. In light of the view that Welty takes about women's issues, is there any significance in analyzing her fiction from the perspective of female independence? Thinking of her statement not only about her own works, but also about the purpose of literature and art in general, is there justification in discussing fiction by Welty, Chopin, and Porter from this particular viewpoint? What mode of approach will enable readers to discuss their fiction from a feminist perspective, without distorting the authors' original intentions and the textures and implications of the texts? Furthermore, more importantly, if such an approach can be attained, can it still avoid being vague, evasive, and irresponsible? Is Welty's stance irresponsible and anachronistic? Is it her posture for encasing herself in the role of an artist simply advocating an art-for-art's-sake principle? Is she indifferent and detached? All these considerations arise from seeing her detestation of the women's rights movement. In this age when a feminist approach is prevalent in the field of literary criticism as well as in other fields and spheres, in a superficial reading, some of Welty's flat and plain statements are baffling. However, the reading of all of her statements on women's issues in *Conversations with Eudora Welty* and *More Conversations with Eudora Welty*, and particularly, "Must the Novelist Crusade?" and above all, the close reading of her stories, clarify these questions. Although Welty wrote "Must the Novelist Crusade?" in response to the queries she received as a Southern writer on racial issues, it bears a great significance and relevance for feminist criticism. The reading of it makes readers realize that it is quite justifiable to discuss her stories from a feminist perspective. Moreover, it enables readers to see what feminist criticism and literary works about women and by women can achieve for women's issues.

As is strikingly revealed in "Must the Novelist Crusade?" Eudora Welty is far from being indifferent and irresponsible, despite her seemingly reserved and curt comments on women's issues. Rather, she is "passionately concerned," and is keenly aware of the role of writers, when it comes to issues in society (154). Referring to how Turgenev's stories caused the Czar to feel moved to free the serfs in Russia, Welty insists that writers achieve more power to move when they express "firsthand" what they have seen than when attempting to write what she calls "inflammatory tracts" (156). She states resolutely how far writers are from being indifferent: "Indifference would indeed be corrupting to the fiction writer, indifference to any part of man's plight. Passion is the chief ingredient of good fiction. It flames right out of sympathy for the human condition and goes into all great writing" (156).

Despite her sincere and deep concern and sympathy for all human plights, Welty still does not actively advocate what she calls "causes" of racial or women's issues, *because* as a passionately concerned writer, she is too perceptive and conscientious to categorize people, conditions, and issues under any "labels" and "generality" so as to make them cater to any "cause" (148, 150). She states: "We cannot in fiction set people to acting mechanically or carrying placards to make their sentiments plain. People are not Right and Wrong, Good and Bad, Black and White personified." "Fiction writers cannot be tempted to make the mistake of looking at people in the generality." "The first act of insight is to throw away the labels" (150). Applying her terms to the analysis of stories from the perspective of feminine independence, one cannot categorize and divide character, writers, and readers into Women and Men, Feminist and Non-feminist, etc. As has been mentioned in the introductory chapter, the study of the stories by Welty, Chopin, and Porter from the perspective of feminine independence and isolation makes readers realize that patterns of feminine independence observed in their stories cannot be categorized simplistically. Welty states, "Characters in fiction" "are individuals every time" (150). The actions, vicissitudes, and thoughts of each female character examined in this chapter are manifold. Each story and plot differs one from another, and characters *are* "individuals" "every time," using Welty's terms (150). None of their predicaments and successes serves to prove plainly either benefits or vices of either feminism or anti-feminism. None of the characters, when they do at all, successfully attains independence without great struggle, for instance. When they fail to be independent, they still always leave readers pondering deeply over their potential to achieve independence and self-realization.

These complexities of the theme of female independence and isolation prove a point by Welty: "There is absolutely everything in great fiction but a clear answer" (149). This clearly echoes the observation made in Chapter 3 on her "A Curtain of Green." In this story, Welty does not present the beauty and the solacing effect of the rain on Mrs. Larkin as a clear answer or a solution for her tragedy. In "Must the Novelist Crusade?" Welty asserts what fiction does not do and what it is not about. It does not present a clear answer. It does not argue. Welty says that arguments aim at "neatness," whereas fiction writers must confront "confusion" as they aim "to show" and "disclose" life (149). She insists that, although fiction is highly organized, "it is organized around anything but logic" (150). Fiction does not prove. Welty says that if one attempts to prove, one novel will settle it, and there need not be numerous novels by different writers. There is more diversity in what novels attempt to capture than one can "prove" (151). Therefore, no novel is like another. Welty maintains that writers do not "correct," "condone," and they do not even "comfort" by any means, but "make what's told alive" (152). Passionate and conscientious attempts of individual writers necessarily exclude all of these directions that Welty lists as what fiction is not about. What is common in these items is that all of them result from being driven by temptations to solve clearly once and for all. Even when a novel deals with women's problems, and when criticism takes a feminist approach, their methods are not the same as those of propaganda, and their aim is not, using Welty's terms, to "answer" or "correct" (149, 152).

If the task of writers is not to solve, then, what do they achieve at all? In presenting "confusion" of life instead of "neatness," and in refusing to "answer," "correct," or even to "condone" and "comfort," do they separate themselves from the dire needs for problems to be answered, solved, and corrected, and for the suffering to be comforted (149, 152)? Are they so driven to pursue the Muse that they use suffering as their material? Rephrasing Welty's assertions, the reason writers do not "answer," "correct," or "comfort" even when they are deeply concerned is because such attempts in writing only destroy, instead of answering, correcting, or comforting, despite the seriously good intentions of such endeavors (149, 152). In writing, writers paradoxically achieve more of such intentions *when* they do *not* aim to, at least, not in ways "crusaders" mean by these terms (146). When writers try to solve, answer, correct, or comfort, they destroy what they depict and the relationships between writers and readers, and the characters and the readers. Summing up her assertions in "Must the Novelist Crusade?" Welty ponders over the present day situation and these relationships. She writes:

> How can one kind of relationship be set apart from the others? Like the great root system of an old and long-established growing plant, they are all tangled up together; to separate them you would have to cleave the plant itself from top to bottom. (155)

If they try to prescribe solutions and comforts for problems of a society and individuals, writers will have to split relationships, emotions, situations, that is, everything they attempt to depict, and separate them from their roots. Likewise, if literary critics aim to wring out a "solution" from the act of analyzing stories in the way propaganda does, for instance, for women's problems, they will destroy the stories as art (151).

Avoiding temptations to "answer," solve, or to "prove" and "argue" clearly, writers allow and struggle with "overflowing" "profuse" myriads of possibilities that can hardly be regulated when they are at work (149, 151). Cheryll Burgess aptly compares this assertion of Welty about writing and writers with the uncontrollable, overflowing garden of Mrs. Larkin and the meaning of Mrs. Larkin's struggles in it (Burgess 136). Like Mrs. Larkin, writers deliberately allow possibilities to multiply and compound (Burgess 137). Burgess quotes Welty's "How I Write," in which Welty mentions the constant, overflowing, ever-changing force of the possibilities of stories that writers face and deal with, whose mystery can never be dealt with by any attempt to control or even to fathom them. Welty emphasizes in "How I Write" as well as in "Must the Novelist Crusade?" that writers' and artists' role is not to try to control or to solve them ("How I Write" 242). Like Mrs. Larkin, the more overflow writers allow, the more they struggle. Only through rigorous and assiduous strivings does a writer express, at all, what Welty calls "his own moral principles" ("Must the Novelist Crusade?" 152). The same applies to criticism and interpretation. Even when taking a feminist perspective, for instance, in reading and analyzing literary works, readers still allow "overflowing" "possibilities" that a text keeps presenting "by the minute" like a kaleidoscope, and struggle with them.

Another significant aspect of writing that Welty points out is that "moral convictions" of writers are "implicit," "deep down," and "private." Unlike the methods of crusading, it requires "quiet," instead of loudness and the presence of the masses (153). Again Welty's point is not to shelter writers and to exempt them from the responsibilities of having expressed any "moral principle." Again Welty mentions the destructive effect of the methods that are not appropriate for writing. She points out that the measures for catering to causes and addressing the masses are alike and loud, and thus, drown individual voices. She points to the ironical consequence: "Enormities" of individual experiences "can be lessened and cheapened," instead of revealed (153). In Welty's opinion, fiction surpasses the addresses to a crowd. According to her, the privacy of a writer and the individuality of a character whose exact match is never found give much more intensity to depicted experiences, and thus, impress more, and address more than crusading for a crowd and a cause. Likewise, a "moral conviction," for instance, of feminist criticism is, using Welty's terms, "implicit" and "deep down," rather than plain and loud (153). But this view does not let critics evade their social and moral responsibilities. They can preserve and bring to light more of the intensity that texts potentially bear when they analyze in "the quiet" and in an "implicit" manner than when making interpretations plain enough to function as propaganda (153). Like writers, they paradoxically achieve more, for instance, for women's issues, when they are keenly perceptive of the complexities of the experiences of individual female characters than when they are convinced of only one clear solution.

Among Chopin, Porter, and Welty, Chopin wrote most explicitly on women's issues, such as the lack of freedom for women and their unfulfilled desire for self-realization. However, her stories on these issues escape being plain propaganda for women's issues because of striking diversities and intense individual experiences that she successfully captures in each of them. One of the issues that she often treats in her stories is the enormity of the psychological impact on women caused by the lack of economic independence. As a writer, Chopin is more capable of illustrating complex psychological conflicts of women than writers of what Welty calls "inflammatory tracts" (156). For instance, Chopin often depicts the situations of female characters who are members of very wealthy families and who yet suffer from serious dissatisfaction. The problems for such women would be grasped much more accurately in literary works through a writer's observation than by propaganda. Their problems would not be considered serious and agitating enough to be the subject matter for a "crusader." They are not as obvious as some other types of women's problems, although they are significant enough for deeper consideration of women's issues.

Needless to say, Edna Pontellier in *The Awakening* is a representative among Chopin's wealthy, discontented female characters. Too obviously, Edna does not suffer from any material lack. Although she is annoyed by the burden imposed on her as a mother and wife to take care of her children, her husband is wealthy enough for them to hire nannies. Although she detests the lack of freedom of her situation, the women of her class in the vicinity in Louisiana all enjoy a leisurely way of life. Despite all these material merits of her life, Edna is psychologically dissatisfied and commits suicide in the end. The unhappiness and suicide of a woman with such affluence and leisure as Edna would have caused hardly any sympathy from ordinary readers, had it not been for Chopin's descriptive power and perceptive viewpoint as a writer. Chopin succeeded so effectively in describing the severity of the lack of spiritual and artistic freedom for Edna that *The Awakening* has become a hallmark for feminism in American literary history.

In *The Awakening*, Edna attempts to establish her own studio. The studio symbolizes Edna's protest against the lack of, and her struggle to win, spiritual and artistic freedom and autonomy, although her rebellion in this form ends only as a feeble attempt. Despite her transient and meager freedom in the studio, Edna fails to establish what Virginia Woolf called a need for women to have a room of their own for them to write, which stands for spiritual and artistic freedom and autonomy as well as actual physical space. Edna fails to gain the vitality needed to free herself and to create. She gives up in the end, and chooses to die.

"Miss McEnders" by Chopin is also a story about a psychologically unfulfilled woman from a wealthy family. In the case of Miss Georgie McEnders, aged twenty-five, the lack of moral freedom and autonomy causes her dissatisfaction. As a daughter of Horace McEnders, a sumptuously wealthy man, and a fiancé of Meredith Holt, a worldly, cheerful man, Georgie is, and will be, economically entirely dependent on a man at each phase in her life. She presently does not work, and will not after marriage, either, as a dependent of her father in her childhood and adolescence, and of her husband from young adulthood on.

Such was a typical and desired way of life for women of her class at the time. Her dependence on them for living a luxurious and leisurely life robs Georgie of vitality and the right to assert certain moral principles in an integrated and consistent way. Despite her moral zeal in certain matters in society, her entire life is ironically sustained by the wealth that Horace McEnders obtained in the dishonest business of the Whisky Ring, and by the wealth of the materialistic and hedonistic Meredith Holt.

The most severe irony that Chopin captures in the story is that Georgie McEnders is totally ignorant of how her father and her fiancé are corrupt, and that her pleasant life rests on the wealth obtained through measures that she would so strongly disapprove of, had she known. Her complete ignorance of the immorality of her father and fiancé does not necessarily reflect her own lack of morality, but definitely reflects the extent of her complete dependence on them. She not only entirely owes them her living, but also is exempted from responsibility to know at all how the family income has been obtained. She is completely dependent on them morally as well as economically, without realizing that she is. Her mode of living is so free of the worry and strife that ordinarily are major parts of making and managing living that she not only does not need to toil for a living, but she also does not need to tend moral questions concerning the source of family income. The exemption from the responsibility to know, however, deprives her of the right to know as well.

In this sense, Georgie is isolated and estranged from what her father and fiancé do. On the surface, she is a privileged member of a wealthy family, but she is neither demanded nor allowed to even remotely participate in what male bread-winners do. Her isolation from the male members of her family directly reflects her isolation from the structure of ordinary society in which men control commerce. Like other women of her set, Georgie is merely an ornament for the male members of her family. Although Georgie is by no means ill-treated by them and is rather fully allowed to live a comfortable, luxurious life, she is deprived of the opportunity to live and act as a free person with initiative and integrity.

Her economic and moral dependence on, and isolation from, the male members of the family would not have been so serious, had she been totally uninterested in conditions of society. The second major layer of irony that Chopin captures in the story is that, like many other women of her set, Georgie is actively interested in morals in society despite her own separation from, and ignorance of, the ordinary structure and commerce of society. Chopin illustrates, with a touch of humor, but sharply, how her idealism is superficial and hypocritical, and ironically based on ignorance.[1] Georgie and other women of her class are actively engaged in activities for investigating and reforming conditions of society, *because* they, especially Georgie, have "ample wealth and time to squander" as well as "a burning desire to do good" (205). Georgie has so much spare time and energy because her life is completely free from any care for making and managing daily life. She practically has nothing to do except daily doing "an elaborately simple toilet" and waiting for her "very elaborate trousseau" to be completed (204). Such matters, however, are not enough to occupy the time and mind of a young, healthy person, so she goes around town in a pretty carriage, one of her personal possessions, which a coachman drives, and eagerly joins in various activities to occupy herself. One afternoon, her "engagement list" reads: "Two o'clock—look up M. Salambre." "Three-thirty—read paper before Woman's Ref. Club. Four-thirty—Join committee of ladies to investigate moral condition of St. Louis factory-girls. Six o'clock—dine with papa. Eight o'clock—hear Henry George's lecture on Single Tax" (204). Her participation in these activities is her attempt to compensate for her lack of opportunity to participate in anything influential and meaningful in society.

However, no matter how ardent she is in these activities, her participation in them still does not allow her to have any worthy influence in society, and she remains isolated. The male members of her family fully allow her to be active in clubs and meetings as much as she likes, because they know that these activities of women bear no substantial influence on the social structure on which capitalistic commerce is based. Horace McEnders and Meredith Holt can completely ignore what Georgie deals with in committees as mere idle engagements of women. As long as the activities occupy women and keep them happy, and consequently keep their mouths shut when it comes to the matters of direct significance for the social stratum and commerce, the men do not pay attention to whatever is discussed by women in meetings. The point is to keep women excluded and isolated from anything socially substantial. For Horace McEnders and Meredith Holt, as long as Georgie remains a docile daughter and a fiancé, it does not matter what she is interested in and does in committees. In their eyes, Georgie is docile, sweet, and lady-like enough as a daughter and a fiancé. She writes in the engagement list of an afternoon, "dine with papa," and places the "framed photographs" of two of them on the table in her room and polishes them "one after another with a silken scarf which is near" (207). Her engagement list shows that the activities she considers as important and beneficial for society are, contrary to her own perception, merely on the same level as being taken out to dine with her father, when it comes to whether they truly have any influence on society and whether they provide a fulfilling and vital meaning for her life.

The problem of Georgie McEnders is that there is a serious gap between what she likes to be and wants to do, and what she actually is. There is also a serious gap between what she likes to be and what the male members of her family want her to be. Georgie has a certain self-image and idealism that she wants to live up to. However, her self-image is completely shattered when she finds out at the end of the story that her existence has been sustained by wealth obtained through immoral measures. Mademoiselle Salambre, who works on Georgie's fancy dress, comes to suggest to Georgie that the wealth of the McEnders might have been obtained immorally. Georgie has dismissed Mlle. Salambre from the making of her trousseau on the grounds that Mademoiselle has an illegitimate child. Mlle. Salambre's point, which is also the essential point of the story, is that it is questionable whether Georgie's life is morally immaculate to the extent that she has a right to dispense a moral judgment on others, for instance, on a person with an illegitimate child. As Lewis Leary observes, "Miss McEnders" is about "the awakening" of Georgie (xi). She is awakened to the harsh truth about the gap between her moral idealism and the reality of her family.

At the end of the story, she is tested on to what extent she can regain her initial purpose and idealism. The author does not present a conclusion about what Georgie chooses to do after her "awakening." It is only told that Georgie throws the flowers sent to her by her fiancé into the fireplace without hesitating a moment, immediately after the revelation of the truth about the source of her family's wealth. "Then she sank into a chair and wept bitterly" (211). Will she now break away from her father and fiancé so that she can continue to pursue moral idealism in a more consistent way? Or, will she choose to discard all of her ideas about moral correctness, and settle to remain the daughter and wife of hedonistic, dishonest men so that she may continue to keep up the luxurious living standard she is used to, and at least stop being a hypocritical idealist? Most likely, she will not be able to make either of these choices. She has lived too dependently on the male members of her family and has received no practical training for earning money herself to begin to live independently. On the other hand, her mind has grown too morally oriented to now totally consent to immoral and hedonistic material pursuits of her father and fiancé and to remain entirely happy with them.

She is likely to become a solitary person who cannot entirely commit to either of the totally conflicting directions. The revelation of the truth about her father's dishonest business awakens her also to her isolated situation. It is now impossible for her to continue to respect and adore her father and fiancé as before. She can no longer feel complete affinity with them. Her happy days as a docile, obedient, sweet daughter and fiancé are over. Even if she might not be able to completely break away from the bond with them, there will be serious discord between her and them from now on. On the other hand, she finds herself isolated from those whom she used to consider as comrades, working together for the betterment of society. "Her heart was beating violently" and "her cheeks were flaming" when she found out that everybody in town knew of her father's crooked business, including her "coworkers, who strove with her in Christian endeavor" (211).

Although Chopin by no means favorably treats the bourgeois life and prudishness of Georgie McEnders, it is still possible to discern in Georgie some elements of a woman who would rather work actively in society than remain only a daughter and a wife. Although her self-image is false and ironically emphasizes the gap between her ideal and reality, it shows her a potential that is not fully developed because of the circumstance she has been placed in. On the table in her room, she places "books, pamphlets, and writing material" (207). It represents her self-image—that she is an intellectual person who actively reads, writes, and acts for the betterment of society. Although, in reality, she is far from truly achieving the aim which she pictures in her mind, at least she wishes to be intelligent and active. One of the reasons she likes Meredith Holt is because, in her perception, he is "likely to interfere in no way with her 'work'" (208). Georgie wants to think of herself as a woman who has significant and influential "work" in society (208). The most significant action that Georgie takes within her limitation as a daughter of a corrupt bourgeois family and that reveals her undeveloped potential is that she goes out to find out herself the truth about her father's business. When Mlle. Salambre insinuates that Georgie's family might be stained by immoral acts in the past, "a sudden, wild, defiant desire" assails her "to test the suggestion" (210). She decides to go out to the streets and to ask passers-by about the McEnders family without letting them know that she is their daughter. It was time for her to go to another of her committees, "but she would meddle no further with morals till her own were adjusted, she thought" (210). The result of her inquiry with several passers-by is that every person in town knows of McEnders' corrupt business. This revelation is a great shock for Georgie, but at least, she does not shrink from exposing herself to the revelation and to awaken herself to the truth that would be most unpleasant and disheartening for her. Even though the revelation will mean the total collapse of everything on which she has based her life and ideas, and she might not know the way out from the impasse she will have to face, she would rather know the truth than continue to "meddle with morals" with her own remaining so crooked (210). Georgie's character is at least upright enough to realize the necessity to consider her own moral position if she is to judge the moral conditions of others at all. She dares take a step to her own "awakening."

In "Elizabeth Stock's One Story" we see another portrayal by Chopin of a female character whose potential is not fully realized. The conclusion of "Elizabeth Stock's One Story" is as dismal as that of *The Awakening*, but the author commends the potential of Elizabeth Stock and depicts how her life ends up wasted. Chopin treats Edna in *The Awakening* and Elizabeth Stock more favorably than she depicts Georgie McEnders. Although it is not impossible to discern the potential of Georgie McEnders, the author presents very little of what Georgie actually does that shows her potential, other than her "awakening" to and resentment of the truth about her family. Among Edna Pontellier, Georgie McEnders, and Elizabeth Stock, Elizabeth Stock exhibits most of the potential of an independent, working, creative woman, although her potential remains at a primitive level and is completely crushed in the end. Unlike Edna and Georgie, Elizabeth Stock, aged thirty-eight and unmarried, has work experience, having been a post-mistress in the village of Stonelift for six years. While Elizabeth has this job, she is economically independent. She is dismissed from the position, the loss of which is what the narration given by Elizabeth in first person is about. Reading her rendition of what happened to her, readers see that the job has been significant and that being dismissed from it was fatal for her. As the incident that she narrates unfolds, she is quite devoted to her mission as a post-mistress, although there may be nothing glorious about the position of a post-mistress in a small village.[2] She has been generally content with her life and has had modest self-esteem.

Other than her job experience as a postmistress, one significant characteristic of Elizabeth's life is, as she mentions ardently, her strong interest in writing. In the very first line of her narration, she says: "Since I was a girl I always felt as if I would like to write stories" (586). Her keen inclination to writing has been known to others in the village, as the frame narrator, not entirely sympathetic, tells what people there think of her: "they say she was much given over to scribbling" (586).[3] When the frame narrator examines her desk after her death, he finds it is "quite filled with scraps and bits of writing in bad prose and impossible verse," with "the whole conglomerate mass" of what she has written (586). Nancy A. Walker observes in "Her Own Story: The Woman of Letters in Kate Chopin's Short Fiction" that "Elizabeth Stock's One Story" is about a "proud, independent woman, aspiring writer, whose sense of responsibility to others brings about both her professional and physical down-fall" (Walker 224). [4]

"Elizabeth Stock's One Story" is a story of a solitary person whose voice and ambition are suppressed, and whose life is destroyed.[5] Like Georgie McEnders, Elizabeth Stock is isolated from the mainstream of the commercial and social stratum. She is also kept completely ignorant of what actually goes on in the society she lives in, although the experiences of Elizabeth and Georgie are quite different. Georgie is ignorant of how her luxurious life is sustained, while Elizabeth is ignorant of how the security of her meager, modest position is controlled by the people beyond her reach and how insecure that status is. Elizabeth fails to discern that Nathan Brightman and Collins, the influential men in power in the village of Stonelift and St. Louis, respectively, plot to discharge her from her position so that they can give the position to the son of Collins. But Elizabeth would not likely to be able to deal with their scheme even if she knew. The irony is that she takes the trouble to carry the postcard from Collins to the house of Brightman in which Collins urgently summons Brightman so as to discuss the position in the post office of Stonelift and to decide to fire Elizabeth and hire Collins' son. The train that brings mail to the village is late that particular day due to bad weather, so people have already gone home and have not received their mail. When the train finally comes and Elizabeth begins to sort mail, by chance, she happens to glance at the postcard from Collins to Brightman. When she is at home, she cannot help thinking that, if the postcard does not reach Brightman that day, he will miss the meeting, and so she decides to go back to the office and to take the mail to Brightman. The most severe irony of her fate is that the walk to the Brightmans' that night in the bad weather causes her to become ill and to die from consumption in a few months and lets Brightman use the fact that Elizabeth reads the mail of others as one of the reasons to fire her. When she dies, she already knows that she has been fired and that the son of Collins has replaced her.

The entire narration of "Elizabeth Stock's One Story" is structured to suppress Elizabeth's voice.[6] She tells her story in a way that lightens the gravity and critical tone of her true voice. She always hastily adds apologetic, moderate comments after expressing her true feelings and thoughts. This mode of narration reflects how she has always suppressed her true self to manage her living in the small village. She has tried to avoid being too isolated in the community and among her relatives. However, in the end she dies from consumption as an isolated person in "the incurable ward" in the St. Louis City hospital (586). In addition to being suppressed, her voice is completely silenced in the end when she dies.[7] The unsympathetic frame narrator considers the way she dies acceptable because, especially towards the end, verbally, Elizabeth expresses very little of her opinions and emotions. The frame narrator comments on her dying process: "There were no unusually pathetic features attending her death. The physicians say she showed hope of rallying till placed in the incurable ward, when all courage seemed to leave her, and she relapsed into a silence that remained unbroken till the end" (586). The social dynamics of the community of Stonelift isolate her, exclude her, silence her, and get rid of her, in robbing her of her job, her income, her health, her life, and her voice, and destroy her potential as a writer.[8]

Elizabeth's narration consists of camouflaged accounts of how she loses her job, her savings, her health, her ambition, and finally her life, one by one, when she is thirty-eight, and of her own feelings about each of these fatal losses. First, being fired from the job is a major shock in her life to the extent it becomes an incentive for her to finally write "One Story" about it. She describes the shock after explaining her sickness after her trip to the Brightmans: "When one morning, just like lightning out of a clear sky, here comes an official document from Washington, discharging me from my position as postmistress of Stonelift. I shook all over when I read it, just like I had a chill; and I felt sick at my stomach and my teeth chattered" (590). She asks Vance Wallace, one of her acquaintances who happens to be at the office, what it means, "when you can't understand a thing because you don't want to" (590).[9] However, she does not express her utmost grief to the full. She immediately adds that it was her fault that led to the dismissal, which is an unnaturally humble, apologetic, self-effacing statement. Before she dies, she writes in her hospital room: "But now that I got my pen in my hand and sitting here kind of quiet and peaceful at the south window, and the breeze so soft carrying the autumn leaves along, I feel as I'd like to tell how I lost my position, mostly through my own negligence, I'll admit that" (587). When she tells who replaced her and the dynamics that enabled him to get the position, she adds comments to show potential readers that she has nothing against the person. However, to objective readers, that is, to readers outside the community of Stonelift whose lives are completely uninfluenced by the political dynamics of the village, it is quite obvious that Elizabeth has been sacrificed to political favoritism. Elizabeth describes the person as "a kind of delicate, poetical-natured young fellow that can't get along in business" (590). She notes, "they used their influence to get him the position when it was vacant. They thinks it's the very place for him. I reckon 'tis. I hope in my soul he'll prosper. He's a quiet, nice-mannered young man" (590-91). When Vance Wallace and some people in the community think of boycotting him, she admonishes them. "I told them they must be demented, and I up and told Vance Wallace he was a fool" (591). Throughout the entire narration, we see that she always attempts to sound as if she thinks the needs of others have priority over her own needs. Even if the son of Collins takes away her position, she feels she should hope for his happiness and should think that the people who want him to give the position back to her are not in their senses.

Another instance of her self-sacrifice is her financial support of her nephew, Danny. What is serious for her about having helped him is that by the time she is terribly sick, she can no longer afford to do what the doctor recommends her to do, that is, she cannot afford to spend the winter in the South (591). Yet, she feels that she should make sure to avoid sounding as if she regrets what she has done for the nephew. She says that he seems like the only capable son of her sister and so ambitious about studying that she "would have felt sinful" if she does not help him to go to school (591).

Of all the things she does, her act of bringing the postcard to Brightman in the bad weather has been her utmost self-sacrifice. However, she does it most likely because he is the man in power in Stonelift. Although Elizabeth is not the type of person to be keen about winning the favor of a politically powerful person, as one of the members of the small community she cannot entirely escape the impact of Brightman's actions. We see another instance of her adding a comment to soften the critical tone of her statement in her description of the smallness of the village. At first she gives her honest observation and feeling. "Often seems like the village was most too small; so small that people were bound to look into each other's lives, just like you see folks in crowded tenements looking into each other's windows" (587). However, she immediately adds: "But I was born here in Stonelift and I got no serious complaints. I been pretty comfortable and contented most of my life" (587).

Although her enthusiasm for writing is her chief characteristic, as is indicated by the frame narrator's introduction of her as "much given over to scribbling" and by mentioning first in her self-introduction that she was always interested in writing, she adds quite a few comments about her meager writing ability (586).

Finally, when she describes the end of her own life, she adds a comment to make what she has just expressed sound less grave, even though the process of dying from consumption after being fired is a desperate situation for her. First, she says: "But indeed, indeed, I don't know what do to. Seems like I've come to the end of the rope" (591). Then her description of the day in the hospital echoes what she says about the quiet and the peaceful weather in the beginning section of the narration: "O! it's mighty pleasant here at this south window. The breeze is as soft and warm as May, and the leaves look like birds flying. I'd like to sit right on here and forget everything and go to sleep and never wake up" (591). Although this is her true feeling at the end, she adds finally, and closes her narration and life for good: "Maybe it's sinful to make that wish. After all, what I got to do is leave everything in the hands of Providence, and trust to luck" (591). Till the last moment of her life, she does not stop acting according to the norm designated as desirable by society, thinking about what she ought to do, and criticizing herself when her true feelings deviate from what is thought desirable by others. So she attempts to conclude her story as a pious, submissive, quiet person who does not trouble others and who submits to religious resignation.

Although Elizabeth Stock fails in everything in the end and dies as an isolated, ostracized person, out of her isolated and very much restricted circumstance, she clearly announces her potential as a writer, although under the disguise of humility. Finally feeling that she has come up with something worthwhile to write a story about, she records the injustice done to her despite her exasperating effort to deliver a postcard. It is her narrative strategy to mix enough mild, disguised, apologetic comments within her real voice, so that she may safely express at least some of her real voice. She keeps modifying the expression of her desperation for the narration to be acceptable to potential readers, especially to those from the community of Stonelift. Although her life and career as a working person and writer may have been not only meager but also are completely destroyed in the end, she summons her remaining strength left to write her "One Story." In the form of "one" seemingly insignificant "story" which the frame narrator condescendingly describes as "the following pages which bore any semblance to a connected or consecutive narration," Elizabeth makes a final assertion of her own rights that have been completely impinged and of her own creativity, just before she dies (586). Her "One Story" becomes her will about her wish, her pride, and her ambition as an integrated person and a writer that are all destroyed by the political dynamics of the small community. She does finally create in the utmost isolation of dying from consumption by herself in the incurable ward of a hospital. Although there is nothing hopeful about her circumstances in the end, what she does in that final and dismal isolation is to write. All through her life she feels that her various attempts at writing have not been entirely successful because she has failed to think of a plot that is unique enough. Finally on her deathbed, she says, "I got my pen in my hand," and says that she will tell how she lost her job, the narration of which will be very unique (587). At her deathbed she has *nothing* left except the pen, i.e., her undeveloped potential as a writer. Elizabeth Stock, in her isolated dying process, *does* have a pen, which most isolated, dying persons do not have.

Mrs. Louise Mallard, another of Chopin's female protagonists, in "The Story of an Hour," cannot fully develop her potential, either. "The Story of an Hour," one of Chopin's best known stories, is about the awakening in Mrs. Louise Mallard of irrepressible desire for existential freedom from the dominance of her husband. However, the pathos and irony of the story are most poignant in that Louise Mallard tastes the sense of the possible freedom only for "an Hour" as the title suggests. Her husband, Brently Mallard, whom Louise and others believe has died in a railroad accident, returns home to them an hour after Louise has been informed of his death, the information of his death having been mistaken. The story presents plenty of the duality of Louise Mallard's consciousness, that is, her contentment of having lived as a loved wife and her deep and sincere grief over the information of her husband's death, and her honest sense of rejoicing in the emancipation. However, overall, the latter is too strong to be curbed by the former. Bernard Koloski comments that the brief, free "hour" of Louise Mallard is a "powerful," "startling moment," and "one of the most heavily discussed moments in nineteenth-century American Literature." Koloski observes that many critics have described Louise's "hour" "as a woman's cry of joy over liberation from male dominance" (Koloski 3). As it is emphasized in the story, and as we have observed in similar cases of Edna Pontellier in *The Awakening* and Georgie McEnders in "Miss McEnders," Louise Mallard has never been maltreated by her husband. Contrary to that, he "had never looked save with love upon her" (353). However, it is the nature of that love that is severely questioned and its negative aspect that is emphasized in the story. When Louise Mallard thinks of the years ahead of her that she will spend for herself by herself without the love of her husband upon her, she feels that she will no longer be under "powerful will bending her in that blind persistence with which men and women believe they have a right to impose a private will upon a fellow-creature. A kind intention or a cruel intention made the act seem no less a crime as she looked upon it in that brief moment of illumination" (353). Although Louise Mallard tries to remind herself of her love for her husband, she finds her craving for freedom to be too strong and her love for him to be somewhat questionable. She contemplates: "And yet she had loved him—sometimes. Often she had not. What did it matter! What could love, the unsolved mystery, count for in face of this possession of self-assertion which she suddenly recognized as the strongest impulse of her being!" (353).

In the eyes of those who surround her—her sister, Josephine, her husband's friend, Richards, and her husband—Louise is a frail woman with heart disease. However, it is noteworthy that her frail image is used to describe how impossible it is for her to resist the overwhelming sense of freedom: "she was striving to beat it back with her will—as powerless as her two white slender hands would have been" (353). This line by Chopin overthrows a clichéd stereotype of a woman with a heart problem whose "powerlessness" and "two white slender hands" cannot stand the shock of the news of her husband's sudden death (353). Chopin's modern perception presents an entirely new concept of what a frail woman cannot fight back. When Louise dies at the end of the story upon the unexpected return of her husband, doctors say she has died of heart disease, but it is added "—of joy that kills" (354). Brently's friend Richards' quick move to shield Louise from the sight of her husband has been too late. In the eyes of those around Louise, she dies of too much joy that her husband has not been dead. Louise's true consciousness is revealed only to readers. In the eyes of the readers, she dies either due to the shock that her too strong joy of having been freed from the dominance of her husband is completely, abruptly crushed as false, or due to the too strong joy that she has tasted for an hour. In this sense, the ending of "The Story of an Hour" is ambiguous.

Louise Mallard goes through the brief but intense process of the awakening of self-emancipation literally in isolation. She literally keeps to herself while she immerses herself "in a very elixir of life" of freedom (354). The author accentuates her strict privacy in describing her one hour's experience of freedom for the first—and the last—time in her life. Immediately after she abandons herself to grief over the death of her husband, Louise retreats into her room: "When the storm of grief had spent itself she went away to her room alone. She would have no one follow her" (352). In "The Story of an Hour" Mrs. Louise Mallard's physical withdrawal into isolation at this point in the story marks her departure on her existential pursuit of freedom. When she is by herself in her room, there is, "facing the open window, a comfortable, roomy armchair" (352). When she immediately sinks into the chair that faces outside, having been physically consumed, her self-emancipation begins in the symbolic form of being exposed to the air from outside. Throughout the story, the imagery of the scene and the sounds from outside that Louise sees and hears through the window symbolize freedom to which she is suddenly exposed.

> She could see in the open square before her house the tops of trees that were all aquiver with the new spring life. The delicious breath of rain was in the air. In the street below a peddler was crying his wares. The notes of a distant song which some one was singing reached her faintly, and countless sparrows were twittering in the eaves. There were patches of blue sky showing here and there through the clouds that had met and piled above the other in the west facing her window. (352)

At first her eyes look weary, possibly because of exhaustion, but her awakening is already beginning as she looks "away off yonder on one of those patches of blue sky" (353). Even in her tired eyes, the signs of her awakening are discerned. Her glance at this point shows "a suspension of intelligent thought" rather than merely "reflection" (353). Then, the irrepressible joy of having been freed begins to seize her, and she feels that the sense which she still cannot name and pinpoint is "creeping out of the sky, reaching toward her through the sounds, the scents, the color that filled the air" (353). When she shortly recognizes what besieges her and abandons herself to it, whispering "over and over under her breath: 'Free, free, free!' " dullness and fear disappear from her eyes, and they become "keen and bright" (353). Her exhilaration begins to influence her physical condition, too. Her pulse begins to beat fast, and her blood circulation and her whole body condition suddenly improve: "the coursing blood warmed and relaxed every inch of her body" (353). Such a startling description of the actual physical influence on Louise of the sense of having been freed makes one wonder if the possible cause of Louise Mallard's chronic illness might have been psychological repression because of the lack of freedom. For one hour, Louise continues "drinking in a very elixir of life through that open window" and to imagine the radiant free days with different hues ahead of her: "Spring days, and summer days, and all sorts of days that would be her own" (354). She prays that her life from then on will be long. The description of what she wished "only yesterday" is striking: Yesterday, she "thought with a shudder that life might be long" (354).

However, Chopin ends "The Story of an Hour" more abruptly, ironically, and bitterly than any of her other stories. After having tasted the intoxicating sense of emancipation only for a startlingly short time, Louise Mallard dies. Chopin does not let the heroine enjoy the sense of freedom even for a single whole day, and does not let her go out of her house even a step before she dies. The author makes Louise die, keeping her potential completely undeveloped. Louise's emancipation is entirely symbolic and private. Mary E. Papke points out in her discussion of "The Story of an Hour" that Chopin seems to point out that the conclusion for emancipated women is destruction and dissolution if their emancipation is only private. Unless they are provided the right to actually live out that vision, their self-emancipation will destroy them (Papke 64). In the case of Louise Mallard, society and the expectation of others would require Louise not to be open about her explosive desire to be free. Because Louise awakens to the sense of independence and freedom for the first time in her life when she is informed of her husband's death, she will suffer from harsh reproaches from a society if others know of her joy over being freed. To them it would seem terribly immoral and perverse of Louise to rejoice over her husband's death. It would not occur to them that Louise delights not so much in his death as in her own new freedom. No one around her contemplates what repression she might have experienced in her marriage. The author makes Louise die before society finds out her true thoughts and ostracizes her, without letting her openly express her joy of being emancipated, and lets her taste the joy strictly in isolation. However, because society would not allow her to fully pursue her freedom, the author sought to maximally reveal Louise's desire for freedom by isolating her and allowing her novel experience to take place strictly in her private room. The limitless expansion of the open sky she sees from her window symbolizes the unfulfilled, but limitless, potential of Louise, which the author did not resist expressing even at the cost of isolating her and making her die in the end lest society crushes her. The ending of "The Story of an Hour" is similar to that of *The Awakening* in that the female protagonist dies after pursuing potential freedom symbolically in the expansion of nature, in the open sky and in the vast sea.

Although Edna Pontellier, Georgie McEnders, Elizabeth Stock, and Louise Mallard differ considerably in their degree of hoping for and achieving independence, they all wish to be independent and to establish their autonomy. Edna, Georgie, and Elizabeth aim to pursue their artistic, moral, and creative goals, respectively. Although Louise's emancipation is strictly private and only existential, her craving for freedom is the strongest. Contrary to these women, some of the female protagonists in Chopin's short stories discussed in the chapter, "Passion and Isolation," never aim or wish to be independent. These stories include descriptions of female characteristics that are problematic in light of female independence. Madame Célestin in "Madame Célestin's Divorce," Madame Delisle in "Lady of Bayou St. John," and Mentine in "A Visit to Avoyelles" are all passive, dependent women who never attempt to take any initiative of their own. They never hope to be independent because they are not ready to pay the cost of independence and to be alone and isolated.

The female protagonists in these three stories have the appearance of feminine frailty, but at the core of their hearts, they are hard, practical realists. Madame Célestin, Madame Delisle, and Mentine all appear frail and needing more romantic and affectionate relationships and protection than their present marriages provide. Two of them, Madame Célestin and Madame Delisle almost succumb to the calculating insinuations of Lawyer Paxton and the impassioned words of Sépincourt, a neighbor, respectively, who are not their husbands. Their frail, yielding attitudes lead the male characters to have false hopes and puzzle them. However, when the men find out the gap between what they have been led to dream and what the young wives choose in the end, the inconsistent attitudes that the women have taken make the men feel betrayed, and bring about bitter disappointment on the part of the men. At the core of their hearts, the three women are realists, and choose to stay within the boundary of their present marital status and widowhood that the society would approve of. That they are realistic does not necessarily mean that they are strong. Rather, their realistic side makes them see that they are not strong, and makes them choose to stay in the present status. Their practical nature tells them that they are not strong enough to survive the harsh reproaches that they will receive if they get divorced and marry another man or if they run away immediately after the death of the first husband.

The two opposing reactions of the young married women, i.e., their yielding attitude to almost choose another man and their final persistent attitude in remaining in their status quo, and the gap between their appearance and their final decision stand for the conflict between two possibilities from which these women could choose, the choices the women can make in order to fill their own emotional needs and to avoid being isolated. In one of them, they would satisfy such a need by playing roles as wives and a widow in a community. In the other, they may feel less lonely and less high-strung with a partner who may be more present at home and may tend more to his wife's well-being. The reason why the three women choose the former is, in the interpretation by Peggy Skaggs, they are quite emotionally satisfied with playing the roles in their communities and would rather not lose such roles and approval of the communities. Skaggs observes that these young wives and a widow feel that they can fulfill their need to clearly have their identity by playing esteemed roles (Skaggs 20-22).

Although the three women in question all choose to stay in the assured status as married women and a widow, both choices that are offered to them would have helped them avoid the cost of being isolated, and either way, they are very dependent. Madame Célestin and Madame Delisle, especially, are so dependent that they cannot consistently stick to the status of marriage and widowhood that are already given to them, although in the end they conclude that they will not change their status quo. Their dependent dispositions are deep-rooted. In being faced with the temptation to try different possibilities in which they might be more protected and loved by their new lovers, it never occurs to them what their seeming yielding attitudes to such temptations will cause in the end. They cause painful disappointments and the feeling of isolation on the side of the men who are courting them once they change their minds again and turn them down. They are protected by their present status, and are innocent, or rather, ignorant and childish, in that they are totally ignorant of others' feelings, a result of their preoccupation with only their own mental and social security. They are so deeply interested in only their own welfare that they are clever enough to weigh which is more profitable for them—to remain in the present situation or to run away with other men. They completely disregard the emotional sacrifices they cause in other people's minds. They do not see at all that when their relations with these new men do not work, which is the ending of the stories, these men will be hurt considerably while they would not. They have places to go back to, especially in the case of Madame Célestin, whereas the men do not.

The need for women to be protected and loved, or to put it more accurately, society's tendency to drive women to feel that they need to be protected and loved passively and not to allow them to take initiative to decide, to act and to love results in a morbid upbringing of women. Such education brings up types of women who are so dependent and act in such inconsistent ways whenever any temptation or different possibilities present themselves. Their dependent nature is precisely the cause of their inconsistent attitudes in the face of other possibilities that can possibly result in sacrificing others if they do not act with sufficient thoughtfulness. That is, because they have only grown up with the habit of being dependent, they simply react so passively to whatever outside influences in their present circumstances or future possibilities. They have not developed fundamental simple wisdom such as being able to consider others' emotions, because their upbringing has discouraged wisdom, maturity, and will.

Observing a woman like Madame Célestin, we see a typical result of the morbidity of women's upbringing. She is a prototype of female refinement and ideal domesticity, but as has been mentioned, such education for women, which indeed Madame Célestin has acquired to the point of mastery, has not brought her up to have strength of character or any professional skill to live independently. She takes care of her appearance and her home perfectly. She can always afford to look neat even in the midst of what Lawyer Paxton and she call her predicament, and leisurely sweeps the gallery of her home every morning. It is not entirely the fault of such women that they are that way, because such female refinements and immaculate domesticity are all that they have been brought up for. In a sense, Madame Célestin dutifully performs the tasks that have been assigned her as a woman. No part of the upbringing of women in the period trained them to develop any professional skill. So Madame Célestin is not to be totally blamed for her dependent attitude on men, her own husband or another man, because if her own husband fails to financially support her life, she would not have any skill to support herself. Her small skills such as sewing and giving music lessons are not enough to entirely support her and her children. She has no choice but to depend on somebody else, which usually is simply to depend on a man, if not a present husband, which means that they just marry again. In the conversation between Madame Célestin and Lawyer Paxton we see that they do not value working for women. Both Lawyer Paxton and Madame Célestin herself commiserate so much that she has to work. Lawyer Paxton says, "Here you are, working your fingers off," and the fingertips she looks at on these words of commiseration are so delicate and "rosy" (276). In this scene we see in its entirety the idealization of delicate, fragile, and dependent qualities in women of the period.

Eudora Welty wrote much less explicitly than Kate Chopin on themes of the suppression of women and their need for freedom and self-realization. However, in her short stories that feature female protagonists, we discern the patterns of isolation, independence, and defiance. Her book, *The Golden Apples,* includes two stories, "June Recital" and "Moon Lake," that treat the isolation and independence of a female artist, Miss Eckhart, and the defiance of a female orphan, Easter, respectively. In other short stories discussed in the previous chapter, "Family and Isolation," we discern the problems of femininity and domesticity.

In "Flowers for Marjorie" we observe the problems that the idealized femininity and rigid domestic roles of women cause. As has been mentioned, Marjorie is the epitome of all the supposedly positive elements such as fertility, hope, happiness, wholesomeness, radiance, beauty, softness, and calmness. In her pregnant state, she represents the natural and organic order. All her assets represent qualities of idealized femininity. Supposedly they shall all comfort Howard as a psychological oasis while they live in the dingy, urban environment of New York. As Marjorie sits by the window in their house, every physical detail of her body, i.e., her hair and arms, are beautiful and delicate. Her beauty reminds Howard of his hometown in the South: "It was hard to remember, in this city of dark, nervous, loud-spoken women, that in Victory, Mississippi, all girls were like Marjorie—and that Marjorie was in turn like his home. . . . Or was she?" (194). The question that the author makes Howard ask after the ellipse marks the beginning of the crucial questioning and the subversion of the value of idealized femininity of Marjorie. As has been observed in the previous chapter, all the supposedly positive, feminine assets of Marjorie terribly smother and menace Howard, to the extent that he is driven to murder her. Howard's question whether she was "like his home" or not represents skepticism of idealized femininity in general (194). The question can be paraphrased: "Or are idealized feminine qualities such as beauty, gentleness, etc. really like homes, i.e., the ultimate source of solace, comfort, and happiness (for men)?" Howard's answer to the question is negative. Not only does he not appreciate her qualities, but also he hates her for them and murders her. In general the answer to the question above may not always be positive.

The tension between Marjorie and Howard and his consequent murder of her also make one question whether the rigid division of labor between a man and a woman in a family is the best form for the family's welfare. In the case of Howard and Marjorie, Howard exclusively plays the role of a bread-winner, although he is presently unemployed, and Marjorie exclusively takes the part of bearing a baby and staying home. The strict division of labor between them badly separates the consciousness of the two without functioning to benefit their family life. As has been pointed out, Marjorie's conviction that she is doing her part perfectly, as a woman, in her view, in being soundly pregnant, is quite strong. Out of this conviction and confidence that are overbearing for Howard, she reproaches Howard for staying unemployed. She begins to suspect that Howard has stopped trying to find a job, and whispers to him, "Why, Howard, you don't even hope you'll find work any more" (198). Her remark made in her fullness, contentment, and confidence as a perfect, pregnant woman at this particular point in the story causes Howard to murder her. However, Marjorie is not a ruthless person in reproaching Howard, because, as has been pointed out, in her view, there is nothing she can do about Howard's employment except to hope that he will keep trying and that he will shortly be employed. In her view, the matters concerning bread-winning strictly belong to the men's sphere, and it is unthinkable to interfere with the men's sphere. In this sense, Marjorie is not acting nasty, but simply acting like a True Woman. And what is the consequence of her being such an ideal True Woman? That Howard and Marjorie are unable to cross the conventional boundary of division of labor between a man and a woman shuts them away from broadening possibilities for solving their dire financial difficulty.

In Welty's "A Curtain of Green," also discussed in the previous chapter, "Family and Isolation," we observe another instance of problems that a conventional family life causes. From the description of the mode of living of the women in Mrs. Larkin's neighborhood in Larkin's Hill and what one guesses about Mrs. Larkin's life before the death of Mr. Larkin, we see that the life of the women in Larkin's Hill is typically and strictly that of rigid confinement in the insipidness of conventional domesticity. The women in Mrs. Larkin's neighborhood shut themselves in the confined but protected and safe way of life and are content. However, their problem is that their lives lack vitality and meaningful activities as is symbolized by their separation from the force of nature. Having lived a life devoid of vitality and contact with the outside world and nature, they have failed to develop the appreciation and apprehensiveness of the dynamic vicissitudes of life and nature. As a result, their dispositions have been formed to be rigid and unsympathetic. They fail to genuinely sympathize with the unexpected plight that befalls their neighbors, Mr. and Mrs. Larkin. They fail to sympathize with and will fail to accept any happenings that deviate from the rigid, fixed pattern of life within which they currently confine themselves, and from which any of them might fall out, if a chance misfortune should visit them.

Before the death of Mr. Larkin, Mrs. Larkin may have lived a more or less similar life as that of her female neighbors. In fact, she has been a wife of an honored member of the community, after whose father the town has been named. Mrs. Larkin's problem is that, as a woman whose life has been formed into the fixed pattern of living only as a wife of a dominant citizen so far, when her husband suddenly dies, she is faced with the reality that it is difficult for her to search for an alternative new way to live other than her previous mode of living, although she is courageous enough to launch the search. At the end of the story, she still has not figured out exactly into what sort of new life she should settle, although she is at least relieved from the extreme tension of almost murdering a hired boy, through the soothing effect of rain. Throughout the story, she is called only "Mrs. Larkin," the last name of her husband's family, whereas, as Papke notes, in "The Story of an Hour," Mrs. Mallard begins to be called by her first name, Louise, after her awakening (Papke 62-64). Once a person's fate makes her stray from the fixed role and pattern that are designated by a society as appropriate, she cannot fit in the community anymore. Mr. Larkin's death has changed Mrs. Larkin's situation and status in the community, and the community, being rigidly conventional, has no suggestion how she may live in the community and be accepted by it again. It just leaves her in desolate isolation, aggravating her isolation caused in the first place by Mr. Larkin's death. Given the reality that the kind of misfortune that befell Mr. and Mrs. Larkin is not rare, the fact that the symbolic community of Larkin's Hill has only one fixed mode of life to suggest for women is in no way wholesome for the welfare of its members.

Another story discussed in Chapter 3, "Family and Isolation," "María Concepción" by Porter, also exhibits very problematic patterns of heterosexual relationships. In "María Concepción," women aggravate their isolation, instead of solving it, by having relationships with an ineffectual man. Both María Concepción and María Rosa fail to see that their blind, servile submission to what Juan Villegas demands from each of them does not lead to fulfilled lives for them and only brings about misery. As has been observed, Juan regards María Concepción, not as an individual with an initiative and personal integrity of her own, but merely as a convenient, simple tool that stoically takes care of his daily needs. Juan fails to see that she also is a wholesome human with emotions, thoughts, and plans of her own. Juan tells his chief that he has never used violence toward her, but contrary to his words, he actually attempts to beat her when he returns home from his elopement with María Rosa. His purpose in beating her is an attempt at "reëstablishing himself in his legal household" after his long absence during his elopement with María Rosa (*Flowering Judas* 20). Juan assumes that a man has a right to beat his wife when he has a purpose. His assumption is based on his notion that a man is to rule over his wife in a household. In his view, affairs with other women do not take away from his right as a man to reign in a household. When it is needed, to ensure his reign, one of the effective measures is violence. When María Concepción resists and strikes him back, he is amazed, not realizing the seriousness of his attempt at beating. He does not realize the extent of the psychological wound he has inflicted on her, and merely stares back at her "inquiringly through a leisurely whirling film which seemed to have lodged behind his eyes" (20). The "leisurely whirling film" symbolizes the lack of perceptiveness on his part as to María Concepción's rights such as her need not to be betrayed, not to be beaten, etc. Due to his lack of awareness of the devastating results to which his chauvinistic assumptions have led, his reaction to María's reaction is completely casual and nonchalant: "Certainly he had not even thought of touching her. Oh, well, no harm done. He gave up, turned away, half-asleep on his feet. He dropped amiably in a shadowed corner and began to snore" (20).

Juan despises María Rosa as much as he is disrespectful of María Concepción, although he adamantly persists in indulging himself in pleasure with María, and grieves over her death. In comparing María Rosa with María Concepción who is stoic and silent, he casually commends María Rosa for her merriness. However, that he likes María Rosa a lot because she is not silent and talks does not mean that he truly values her disposition. He condescendingly and casually says, "When she talks too much, I slap her and say, Silence, thou simpleton! And she weeps. She is just a girl with whom I do as I please" (18). He has made a similar type of comment about María Concepción, too: "I say to her, come here, and she comes straight. I say, Go there, and she goes quickly" (18). His comments about the two women show that he regards women as things which he can treat according to his own convenience and desire. When his chief admonishes him about his unfaithfulness to María Concepción, he casually dismisses the subject and says, "as one man of the world to another, 'women are good things, but not at this moment' " (19). He retorts to the warning by his chief, saying, "Let us forget María Concepción and María Rosa. Each one in her place. I will manage them when the time comes" (19). Juan believes that it is men's unquestionable right to view women in the way he does. He is self-conscious of his gender. When he is informed by his chief about the severity of the result of his infidelity to María Concepción, he swells with cocky pride about being desirable to two women both of whose assets he needs: "Juan's expression was the proper blend of masculine triumph and sentimental melancholy. It was pleasant to see himself in the role of hero to two such desirable women" (18-19). This view so much adds to his good mood after having been exempted from being persecuted as a deserter, and makes him feel that the "situation was ineffably perfect, and he swallowed it whole" (19). Juan's attitude appears insipid to another man, his chief, although Juan has talked to him "as one man of the world to another" (19). Already earlier in the story, the nature of Juan has been the object of condescension for his chief, who used to be fond of making fun of Juan for his infidelities. At that time, too, being promiscuous used to fill Juan with masculine pride. On being ridiculed by his chief for his womanizing, he "would laugh with immense pleasure" (11).

Juan's comments on women remind readers of the condescending comment on women by Braggioni in "Flowering Judas." Braggioni confides to Laura: "One woman is really as good as another for me, in the dark. I prefer them all" (154). Although Juan Villegas is not as cunning and calculating as Braggioni, they are quite similar in their unrestrained and self-centered pursuit of their own pleasure. They both are the types who crave being the center of people's attention, although Juan is innocent compared to Braggioni whose cunning makes him more objectionable than Juan. Very much typical of this type, both Juan and Braggioni womanize wildly.

Although it is basically Juan's problem that he does not respect women and regards them only as things that cater to either his domestic or sexual needs, the problematic heterosexual relationships between him and María Concepción and María Rosa are pretty much the fault of the two women, too. Or, the two women have no other choice because of the situation of society. Just as Laura and Braggioni's wife continue to have relationships with Braggioni, both María Concepción and María Rosa subjugate themselves to base treatment by Juan. Of all these four women, María Concepción's reaction to the emotional wound is the most severe and violent. She alone commits murder in order to retaliate for the injustice done to her. At the moment just after she sees Juan and María Rosa flirting, she feels she wants to die, "but not until she had cut the throats of her man and that girl" (8). However, fairly early in the same day, her anger against Juan subsides, and only her anger against María Rosa grows. Eventually, María Concepción penalizes only María Rosa. In the end, María Concepción is completely pacified at the sight of the dead body of María Rosa, feeling that the ultimate cause of the vice has been entirely uprooted and failing to discern that the basic cause of Juan's promiscuity, his nature, has not changed. As is typically seen in her emotional reaction to Juan's extra-marital affairs, María Concepción is a type of a woman who caters to a male-chauvinist social structure and who causes her own gender and herself to suffer and be isolated. She regards only María Rosa, a person of her own gender, as her enemy, and overlooks Juan's conduct. In domestic matters as well as emotional issues, she caters to hierarchical male chauvinism. She is unskeptically proud of being a domestic servant of Juan and his co-workers and despises Juan's chief for not having a "woman of his own to cook for him," and who "moreover appeared not to feel any loss of dignity in preparing his own food" (10). Judie James Hatchett points out that María Concepción subsumes Juan's weakness and deceitfulness in her self-image as a Christian wife (Hatchett 111). Notwithstanding all the treatment of her by Juan, she blinds herself to Juan's shortcomings that have damaged her life, just so that she can continue to pose as a Christian wife. In her view, the status as a church-married woman is so solid that she will be always assured of the role in the community and will never be isolated in it, even if she commits a murder, if the purpose of the murder is to remove the threat to that status. Her own testimony that she is innocent when gendarmes investigate the murder summarizes her view and shows her willing submission to male chauvinism.

> María Concepción heard her own voice answering without a break. It was true at first she was troubled when her husband went away, but after that she had not worried about him. It was the way of men, she believed. She was a church-married woman and knew her place. Well, he had come home at last. She had gone to market, but had come back early, because now she had her man to cook for. That was all. (31)

Although she makes the statement to camouflage her inward fury in order to deceive the gendarmes, it reveals her awareness, and even the acceptance, of what she states as "the way of men." In this statement, publicly, María Concepción permits Juan to have "the way of men," i.e., to womanize and to elope with his mistress as he pleases, and accepts her role as a stoic wife who passively endures emotional damage inflicted upon her.

Hatchett points out that Porter leaves her characters content in making them believe that reality is simple, but that their contentment signals their failure (Hatchett 112). María Concepción's submission to Juan notwithstanding his treatment of her and her contentment to remain his wife after all that has happened represent typical and die-hard causes on the part of women, *their* failure, that cause them to continue to suffer from male dominance under which they are not able to thrive. Feminists may argue that men rule and abuse women—Juan Villegas rules and abuses María Concepción—but women allow themselves to suffer under men's rules, and actually support the social system of male dominance although they may suffer under it.

María Rosa also caters to the value system of a male-chauvinistic hierarchy. Her case is more pitiable than that of María Concepción. Unlike María Concepción, she is not afforded a status and a role in the community even if she pays the cost of allowing herself to suffer from Juan's base treatment. She only disgraces herself and is reproached harshly by the community which regards her murder as permissible as a measure to ostracize her. One possible reason for her to place herself in a position of a mistress is that her erotic relationship with Juan affords her an illusion that she is loved and is not isolated. In the eyes of María Concepción, María Rosa is very much loved by Juan, which, however, is by no means true. When María Concepción sees the dead body of María Rosa, she feels: "María Rosa had eaten too much honey and had had too much love" (28). Although it is only an illusion, the erotic relationship with Juan may have made María Rosa feel that she has her share of "honey" and "love." However, Juan basically regards her as a lower being. To Juan, María Rosa is nothing but a convenient tool for him suited to serve him specifically for his pleasure. While María Rosa is in the army during her elopement with Juan, she plays a base servile role with other women in the battalion, cooking and eating with them "what was left after the men had eaten" (12).

Among the female protagonists of the stories discussed so far whose lives end up wasted, and among Laura and Braggioni's wife in "Flowering Judas" and María Concepción, who all subjugate themselves for different reasons to the most chauvinistic type of male protagonists, María Rosa is the most sorry character, and her lot, the most pitiable. As is typically seen in her weeping when Juan slaps her when he wants her to shut up, throughout the story, she is characterized as a pitiable, weeping female whose lack of strength of character makes her convenient for Juan to use and to do "as he pleases" with. María Rosa does not gain anything by being the way she is. To the contrary, she loses everything as a result, including her life. On her return to the village she is seen "screaming and falling on her face in the road," and is "taken under the armpits by two guards and helped briskly to her jacal" which has been "sadly run down" during her absence (15). In having an affair with Juan Villegas, she has disregarded her occupation as a bee-keeper, too, and has lost her credentials in the community and has become completely isolated in it. To the very end, she keeps weeping. When she is killed, she is heard "wailing in sleep" (28). When investigators come to her jacal with Juan and María Concepción, they see her dead body which has perished entirely without peace and dignity. "The mouth drooped sharply at the corners in a grimace of weeping arrested half-way. The brows were distressed; the dead flesh could not cast off the shape of its last terror. It was all finished" (28). Such is the last lot of María Rosa, who had been introduced in the beginning as "young María Rosa, a pretty, shy child only fifteen years old," and whose "light gay scream of laughter" at first made María Concepción smile and think, "So María Rosa has a man!" (4, 6). Throughout the entire story, the narration is never told from the viewpoint of María Rosa. She and María Concepción destroy the lives of each other over one ineffectual, unworthy man.

In Porter's "The Jilting of Granny Weatherall" we observe an example of a female character who stands up to the adversity caused by betrayal by a man, instead of destroying the life of her own or another. In surviving trying hardships not only for herself but also for other members of the family, Ellen Weatherall completely outgrows John, the husband who passed away early. "She used to think of him as a man, but now all the children were older than their father, and he would be a child beside her" (126). The earlier image of herself as a beautiful "young woman with the peaked Spanish comb in her hair and the painted fan" but weak and leaning on a man and looking up to him "as a man" is entirely forsaken (126). In thinking of seeing John again, she cannot help realize that she did grow and become stronger, that she cannot and does not wish to revert to her previous weaker self. "It seemed strange and there was something wrong in the idea" (126). The present order she has established no longer fits the conventional order of a southern belle leaning on and protected by her beau. In various adversities she experienced, she could no longer afford to remain dainty and to give in to the grief of having been deserted. She dared to outgrow her previous self and the conventional order, while another alternative would have been to remain as she used to be, to let the shock continue to overwhelm her, and to let others take care of her and the household.

Although the stories discussed so far are generally about the unfulfilled lives of the female protagonists and in many cases about their isolation, there are groups of stories by Chopin, Porter, and Welty that are oriented more to the hopeful side of the attempts of female protagonists at self-emancipation. Chopin, who wrote most explicitly of the three writers on the theme of both female emancipation and their failures, wrote numbers of stories that end in hopeful tones as well as many that end in ironical, desperate tones. To mention a few, "Emancipation: Life Fable," "The Maid of Saint Philippe," "Beyond the Bayou," and "A Pair of Silk Stockings" are among the group of stories by Chopin whose endings are more hopeful than some others.

"Emancipation: Life Fable" is an allegorical account of an animal that flees from its cage. At first the animal fears the world outside the cage because it is so unaccustomed to the cage, but by the time it leaps out of it, it begins to live so fully in the outside world that it becomes heedless of the wounds on his sleek sides occasioned in his wild flight. In "The Maid of Saint Philippe" Maríanne spurns the marriage proposal of Captain Vaudry after the death of her father, saying that the "love" and luxurious life in France that the captain speaks of will only rob her of her strength and freedom in the wilderness in America (122). Finally, she walks away, "her brave, strong face turned to the rising sun" (123). In "Beyond the Bayou," La Folle finally leaves the place of her long self-containment on one side of the bayou. As she is awakened to the existence of the new world, she watches "for the first time the sun rise upon the new, the beautiful world beyond the bayou" (180). While the process of emancipation is portrayed through the imagery of the grandeur of the open, expanding nature that is contrasted with the image of enclosure such as a cage, a cultured, indoor life, and a limited area in the stories mentioned above, in "A Pair of Silk Stockings," Chopin compassionately commends little Mrs. Sommers' attempt at gaining freedom in her one-day excursion in a city. In this story she allows herself to use the money she has recently unexpectedly gained for her own humble pleasures such as purchasing a pair of stockings, having coffee and some dainty sweet at a restaurant, and going to a theatre.

"The Last Leaf" and "Old Mortality" by Porter both portray attempts of female protagonists at self-emancipation that do not end in their defeat. The two stories are suited to be discussed in the conclusion of this chapter because they are both about females with exceptionally strong wills who are willing to face the great challenges that are surely to come once they declare their freedom and independence. The tone of their endings is much more hopeful than the stories discussed so far. Especially in "Old Mortality," the quality of the story is quite high in that, while presenting Miranda's departure for the future in a hopeful tone, it also successfully captures the complexity of the nature of her departure. Miranda's future is by no means presented as an assured, complete one. While the so-called declaration of independence by Old Nannie in "The Last Leaf" has a final tone because she is eighty-five years old and declares herself free, so to speak, as a gesture of retirement, young Miranda's journey after her self-emancipation will be much longer and more unsure than that of Old Nannie's, and will not be free of troubles. In the beginning paragraph of "The Last Leaf," "Nannie was prepared to start her journey at once" (*The Leaning Tower* 59). What is meant by "her journey" is her departure from this world, while Miranda's journey after she acclaims her independence will be longer and more winding. Both Old Nannie and Miranda feel that their bonding with others, which was called by the name of "love," has smothered them, and they resolutely mean to break away from them, even at the cost of isolating themselves (*Pale Horse* 87). Miranda, however, later falls in love with Adam Barclay, an archetypical American Adam, who dies from influenza just after Miranda regains consciousness after roaming between life and death in delirium of the fever of influenza. Miranda's career and journey will be full of these dynamic vicissitudes. The significance of "Old Mortality" is that it fully foreshadows the coming of the grave challenges that Miranda is to face, while portraying the resolute and unrestrained will of Miranda to be free from bonding for good.

Old Nannie, a former slave, is finally and for the first time taking repose, shortly before she departs for another world, from her life-long labor. She daily longs for the night to come so that she can rest, "as if all the accumulated fatigues of her life, lying now embedded in her bones, still begged for easement" (*The Leaning Tower* 64). It is now so delicious for her to rest at all because she has never rested in her life. Whenever night comes, "she would sit in the luxury of having at her disposal all of God's good time there was in this world" (64). Her resolution to be free, independent, and to be exempted from the labor of taking care of others, is strong and has a final tone, but she finds immense satisfaction in small matters that represent for her the freedom that she has finally gained. That she finds great pleasure in small matters is indicative of the extent of the lack of freedom she has had in her life during which she has been robbed of even small freedom. When she leaves the house for her solitary cabin, she takes "all sorts of odds and ends from the house," and children are astonished to discover that she "had always liked and hoped to own certain things," because, to them, she always "had seemed so contented and wantless" (60). Once she begins to live alone in the cabin as she wished to, she picks up "making patchwork and braiding woolen rugs" "in the serene idleness" that she has never tasted before (60). In the past, as a "faithful old servant Nannie, a freed slave," she always used to be clad in black and white, but finally as "an aged Bantu woman of independent means, sitting on the steps, breathing the free air," she begins to wear a bandanna of blue color around her head and to smoke a corncob pipe (61). Her enjoyment of these matters reminds readers of little Mrs. Sommers' enjoyment of little things during her one short, free day in Chopin's "A Pair of Silk Stockings."

Miranda's search for freedom is more complicated than that of Old Nannie in that she has many more years to go through than Old Nannie, and more so than those of many female protagonists in the stories discussed so far in that she is more ambitious and has a wider scope than many others. The ending passage of "Old Mortality" is a significant example of the ending of the stories that feature female protagonists.[10] Many of the stories discussed so far end in the death of female protagonists. Edna Pontellier and Elizabeth Stock die as the result of not being able to fit in societies because of their aspiration. Chopin makes Louise Mallard die, just as she is finding her way to freedom. Georgie McEnders is likely to settle into a marriage that will not lead to a fulfilled life for her. The female protagonists in "Madame Célestin's Divorce," "Lady of Bayou St. John," and "A Visit to Avoyelles" remain in the status quo of their marriage or widowhood. In "Flowers for Marjorie" by Welty and "María Concepción" by Porter, female characters are murdered or become murderers due to the adversities of domestic life or a heterosexual relationship. In "The Jilting of Granny Weatherall," Ellen Weatherall dies after her long struggle with domestic predicaments and emotional trauma. Old Nannie in "The Last Leaf" has just freed herself from the bonds enslaving her, but now she is ready for death. Mrs. Larkin in "A Curtain of Green" has many years ahead of her to live independently, but what her life will be like and whether she can survive in a community that does not provide a place for people who have fallen out from the patterns it designates as the norm are to be questioned. "The Maid of Saint Philippe," "Beyond the Bayou," and "A Pair of Silk Stockings" by Chopin present endings for female characters in a much more hopeful tone, but the presentation of the case of female-emancipation in them is less full than the portrayal of Miranda's departure and questioning in "Old Mortality" by Porter.

The ending of "Old Mortality" encompasses the larger scope of fundamental, philosophical questions more than do any other stories. The questions are earnestly posed by Miranda. "Oh, what is life, she asked herself in desperate seriousness?" (*Pale Horse* 87). "What is the truth, she asked herself as intently as if the question had never been asked" (88). In order to seek the answers for these questions, Miranda decides to leave the home she was born and raised in and the marriage she is presently in, both of which she does not feel have provided an answer to her questions, "not in the smallest thing" (85). Her urge to find out the truth for herself is so strong that she is "not sorry for" "feeling homeless" for having departed (84). She says, "I will make my own mistakes," not the ones of those who have surrounded and smothered her (84-85). She fully acknowledges that her future cannot give her promises, false hopes, or a romantic notion, and that she is ignorant, but she declares that she has already taken "a first step" (85). The narration points to her "arrogance," "pride," and "ignorance" as well as her "hopefulness" in describing her determination (84, 89). As Rashmi Gupta notes in discussing Miranda's path, the possible reason why Miranda chooses such a risk in place of a safe and conventional life is because she feels that the previous values have now become "irrelevant" to her current "needs" and that parents' generation has been "indifferent" (Gupta 39, 41).[11] Gupta continues on this point and quotes Margaret Mead. According to the quoted passage, previous generations "cannot conceive of change" and thus only try to pass on established systems and values (Gupta 39). If the orders in the past were still relevant to her new present "needs," Miranda still might have just followed them without skepticism even if they belong to former periods.

Miranda's will and desire for discovering truth for herself by herself are now extraordinarily strong. Her thought of her life as her own has grown so intense that it is described as having been thought "in a fury of jealous possessiveness" (87), and the vast uncertainty and isolation of the path ahead of her does not stop her. Later on, in "Pale Horse, Pale Rider," Miranda is to seek her career in journalism and literature, while experiencing war and the death of her lover, and goes in depth, like Mrs. Larkin in "A Curtain of Green" by Welty, into the questions that she poses at her departure in "Old Mortality." Miranda's departure on the journey to break away from the old system and to find out new truth despite its totally unmapped road at the end of "Old Mortality" is indicative of the psychological strength and the intensity of the character of Miranda, along with the complexity of what she faces. Miranda's energy, determination, and fierceness, along with the uncertainty that she faces, are symbolic of the path of the feminist issue that has been treading its path in "a fury of jealous possessiveness" about its journey being its own (87).

Notes

1. Per Seyersted comments that none of Chopin's stories is sharper in tone than "Miss McEnders." However, Seyersted observes that characterizations are discreet and the irony is softened by humor in "Miss McEnders" (Seyersted 97).

2. Throughout her narration, Elizabeth Stock takes a humble, apologetic, self-effacing tone. In mentioning her strong interest in writing, she adds: "I never had that ambition to shine or make a name" (586).

3. Critics analyzing "Elizabeth Stock's One Story" react strongly to the frame narrator's comment on Elizabeth's interest in writing as her being "much given over to scribbling" (586). They say that this commentary reminds them of Nathaniel Hawthorne's comment earlier in the nineteenth century about the "damned mob of scribbling women" (ex. Nancy A. Walker 224).

4. Nancy A. Walker's guess is that the condescending frame narrator is perhaps a male (Walker 224).

5. Rebecca J. Dickson focuses on and extensively discusses the theme of the suppression and mutilation of women's voice in her dissertation, *Ladies out of Touch: Kate Chopin's Voiceless and Disembodied Women*, although she does not discuss "Elizabeth Stock's One Story." One of Dickson's propositions is that, at the time Chopin wrote, voicelessness characterized women's oppressed lives, that their voices of their internal thoughts, feelings, or artistic longings were suppressed, and that we observe female voicelessness in Chopin's stories.

6. Dickson, pages 57-59.

7. Dickson, pages 118, 147.

8. Dickson, pages 323, 347.

9. Nancy A. Walker suggests that Vance Wallace is Elizabeth Stock's would-be suitor (Walker 225). Toward the end of the story, Vance Wallace says, "I know I'm a fool, Lizabeth Stock," and adds, "I always been a fool for hanging round you for the past twenty years" (591).

10. *Famous Last Words: Changes in Gender and Narrative Closure*, edited by Alison Booth, includes the discussion by Suzanne W. Jones on the ending of "Old Mortality," "Reading the Endings in Katherine Anne Porter's 'Old Mortality.'" Booth observes in the Introduction that many novels present only a few choices for female characters in the end, and that their endings are rarely as varied as the middles of them. Booth points out that in the realistic novels of manners, the female protagonist's prospects are scaled down, and often her penultimate words are contradicted by the fulfillment of a strong communal wish for her romantic union and silence. Agreeing with Nancy Miller, Rachel Blau DuPlessis, and other feminist critics, she observes that the closure of fiction has generally dictated the end of a woman's "ambitious" plot, and that the end of a female "erotic" plot in marriage has an uncanny resemblance to death. Booth points to the premature closure of the female quest plot, and observes that the romance plot leading either to marriage or death predominates (Booth 2).

11. On this point, Gupta refers to the view of a British psychiatrist, David Cooper, who discusses problems of families that cannot deal with the needs of descendants (Gupta 39). Gupta discusses Miranda's choice at length in one of the chapters, "Adolescence in the Miranda Stories," in *Adolescent Hero in the Works of Katherine Anne Porter and J. D. Salinger*, from the perspective of adolescents' psychological struggles and growth.

Chapter 5

Social Issues and Isolation

External social problems such as poverty and racial discrimination frequently cause the most severe cases of isolation. In the previous chapters, the discussion of various states of isolation focused on internal psychological factors of characters and on problematic relationships within a family and between individuals. However, internal psychic and familial factors often closely intertwine with outside social circumstances. Although many short stories by Chopin, Porter, and Welty deal closely with characters' inward states, some of their short stories are clear examples of the treatment of social issues. The three authors are not known typically as addressers of social issues, and the textures and themes of their writing are mostly more internal and artistic than external and social. However, some of their stories that deal with social issues penetratingly address the severity of social problems precisely because the authors are acutely insightful of psychological harm and suffering that social issues cause individuals. The stories by the three authors that will be discussed in this chapter all deal with the major social issues of the American South in the periods when they wrote, such as poverty and racism.

In "The Whistle" by Welty, a fifty-year-old couple, Jason and Sara Morton, are isolated not only from the world outside, but also from each other, because of the apathy they have fallen into due to their destitute living conditions.[1] As sharecroppers in the South, they are entirely at the mercy of Mr. Perkins, an exploitative landlord, who takes away minimum necessities from them.[2] In the particular season when the story takes place, Jason and Sara seriously suffer from the cold climate, because they are provided so little clothing and material for keeping a fire in their shack. During the course of the story, they are forced to cover tomato plants with the minimal clothing that has been left to them to protect the plants from frost, and are left only with thin underwear at the end of the story. Furthermore, they end up burning some furniture in their desperate attempt to kindle the dying fire. Their deprived life keeps being further stripped of whatever has been left to them after the shrill "whistle" of the landlord is heard. The whistle calls his sharecroppers to protect tomato plants at the sacrifice of their own lives.[3]

The utterly piercing cold is the major motif of "The Whistle." Because of the harsh temperature and the bad living conditions, Jason and Sara Morton are almost numb and dumb-founded. They have no spirit whatsoever left to protest and even to communicate their misery to each other. The author emphasizes their isolation from each other as the worst possible emotional consequence of their devastating living conditions. The lack of communication between them now characterizes their relationship. They are "no more communicative in their misery than a pair of window shutters beaten by a storm" (112). Sometimes they spend many days and even weeks without exchanging a word. Their life is "filled with tiredness, with a great lack of necessity to speak" (112). The utter poverty "left them still separate and undesirous of sympathy" instead of uniting them (113). The narrator guesses that, maybe in a remote past, some strong emotion possibly resulting from some discord between them may have caused their present silence, but their silence has now become too constant to imagine that it may have been started by some strong emotion. They are literally frozen in silence and isolation, from which they cannot break away. They utter only one word to each other in the entire story. When the two hear Mr. Perkins' whistle again at the end of the story, Sara says, "Jason . . ." and Jason says in an "uncertain voice" to Sara, "Listen" (120). They say these words in sheer dejection and fright. The curt exchange of only one word to each other at the end of the story signifies that the cold has so completely overtaken their existence that they have nothing else to talk about at all except the cold. They have nothing else to think about except the cold. The cold is so piercing and fierce that it has literally frozen and benumbed them both physically and psychologically. In the middle of the story, Sara "could not help but feel the chill of the here and now, which was not to think at all, but was for her only a trembling in the dark" (115). The cold has robbed them of any meaningful thought as well as their speech. Although Suzanne Marrs believes that the couple regain the memory of their partnership when they stare at the fire together after burning the furniture, Marrs also concludes that such a moment "will not endure" (Marrs 24). Burning the furniture which is the last meager property left to them seems only the final and fatal destruction of whatever minor recourse they possess.

At the beginning of the story, no sound is heard in the habitation of the Mortons except the feeble fluttering fire and the coarse breathing of Jason. Almost throughout the entire story, Jason is heard only breathing in his sleep except when he is awakened by Sara when the whistle blows. The lack of sound in the shack as well as the lack of speech between the two signifies the lack of anything meaningful and comforting in their life. The drowsy sound of the fire and Jason's hard breathing are symbolic of the irreparable exhaustion of the couple and their diminished life. Jason's breathing is slow and utterly exhausted. He "breathed, in and out, slowly and with a rise and fall, over and over, like a conversation or a tale—a question and a sigh" (112). As is seen in Jason's breathing, the verbal capacity of Jason and Sara has been diminished to their hopeless expression of their exhaustion. That they are utterly tired and cold is the only "tale" that they can tell about their life at all and the sole subject matter of any kind of "conversation" they can possibly have (112). Their "tale" of life and their "conversation" are robbed of any recognizable word, and consist only of "a question and a sigh," "a question" over the irrationality of the dejected circumstance and "a sigh" of sheer fatigue (112). In the middle of the story, Jason's breathing grows even more hoarse, and he is "even beyond dreams" (113). The constant rate at which the fire grows weaker is proportionate to the rate that Jason's breathing grows heavier. The difficulty for them to simply keep living continues to grow, and the possibility of their existence continues to diminish every instant. When Sara also finally falls asleep, Jason's breathing continues to grow heavier and heavier, and finally, as a culmination of his isolation, it is "heard by nobody at all" (116). Jason's hard breathing caused by physical malfunction resulting from hard living conditions is unheard and unnoticed by anybody, just as the pounding of the heart of the dying traveling salesman is heard by nobody when he dies in complete isolation in "Death of a Traveling Salesman" by Welty. Both in "The Whistle" and "Death of a Traveling Salesman," the sufferings of the protagonists are completely forgotten by the world. In "The Whistle" the world and the ruthless landlord completely ignore the suffering of the sharecroppers. The weak, helpless people continue to suffer in abject isolation. Nobody protests for them, who have completely lost any spirit to protest at all, because hardly anybody knows of their condition. Just before Jason is awakened by Sara when the whistle blows, his breathing is "cavernous," "like roars coming from a hollow tree" (116). The emptiness and meaninglessness caused by physical and psychological deprivation now characterize the life of the Mortons. The meaning and the reason of their existence are lost to the world. As Marrs mentions, while Mississippi farmers actually did protest politically, Jason and Sara are even deprived of "the energy to engage in protests" (Marrs 21). One could say that they are politically isolated from the world as well as spiritually, all due to the utmost weakness they suffer.

While Welty repeatedly mentions Jason's breathing to describe how exhausted and dejected he is, the author describes how Sara's eyes are full of fear and hollow to show how emaciated she is, too. While Jason is asleep most of the time in the story, Sara is mostly awake with her eyes staring at nothing, being unable to fall asleep. She lies "with her mouth agape, silent, but not asleep" (112). Her gaze is not directed toward anything specific because she is mentally robbed of perceptive capability to focus on anything in particular. Her staring only shows her fright and psychological deprivation. "Her eyes seemed opened too wide, the lids strained and limp, like openings which have been stretched shapeless and made of no more use" (112). Due to the severe living conditions, her senses, including her sight, have lost their function to perceive anything meaningfully. Although Sara and Jason may still see, hear, smell, taste, and touch, the functions of their five senses are "made of no more use" and rendered purposeless because their brains are benumbed and have lost the capacity to mentally process what the senses have caught (112). Just as Jason's breathing sounds "cavernous" and as if it were coming out "from a hollow tree" (116), Sara's eyes are "like openings" with no function (112). Emptiness and meaning-lessness now seize their life and defeat them.

The author also portrays how the meager piece of land and the shack of the Mortons are physically isolated. The place is unnoticed. The author portrays the actual spatial setting of their land and the habitation through a camera-eye visual device. As has been noted in criticism, some omniscient eye, "a closer and more searching eye than the moon's" zooms on the ill-grown, tiny tomato plants (111). The moon, its light white and intense, is described many times as a sole viewer of the miserable circumstance of the sharecroppers. However, its light is far, detached, and objective, and accentuates the isolated circumstance of the small piece of land and the shack. Along with the moon and some omniscient eyes, the author repeatedly employs several motifs to intensify the isolation of the place: the night, the darkness, the calm intensity of the air with no wind, and above all, the extremity of the cold. They all envelop the meager piece of land, the shack, and the existence of the Mortons. At the beginning of the story, the night, the darkness, the moon, and "a closer and more searching eye than the moon's" are introduced in this order as backgrounds to and intensifiers of the Mortons' abject life in the shack (111). "Then the moon rose. A farm lay quite visible, like a white stone in water, among the stretches of deep woods in their colorless dead leaf" (111). "The moonlight covered everything, and lay upon the darkest shape of all, the farmhouse where the lamp had just been blown out" (111).

In the middle of the story, the cold grows more severe after Sara has finally fallen asleep, as the whistle of the landlord awakens her. The moonlight is more intense, and the smallness, insignificance, fragility, and isolation of the farm are more accentuated.

> Every hour it was getting colder and colder. The moon, intense and white as the snow that does not fall here, drew higher in the sky, in the long night, and more distant from the earth. The farm looked as tiny and still as a seashell, with the little knob of a house surrounded by its curved furrows of tomato plants. Cold like a white pressing hand reached down and lay over the shell. (116)

As Jason and Sara are forced out of the bed and out of the shack to the farm outside to cover the plants, their emaciated figures look small and isolated in the surroundings. "Everything was white, and everything looked vast and extensive to them as they walked over the frozen field" (117). After they cover the plants with quilts and what they have been wearing, the motifs are mentioned again to highlight the cruelty of the situation they are placed in. "There was no wind.

There was only the intense whiteness of moonlight. Why did this calm cold sink into them like the teeth of a trap? They bent their shoulders and walked silently back into the house" (118). Whenever they hear the whistle, they listen with "bent heads" (120).

In the middle of the story, a totally different motif of the fruitfulness and the glamour of the fertile seasons in the past is introduced, as Sara imagines these seasons as "a vain dream," while she continues to shiver in the cold (113). However, in the scene of the joyous and bustling commotion of packing harvested tomatoes into cargoes in the town of Dexter in the shipping season, again the figures of the Mortons are small, and ignored. While the commanding figure of Mr. Perkins, whose capitalistic interest and exploitation of the sharecroppers are the causes of the condition of the Mortons, rules the scene, the portion of the crop produced by the Mortons and their figures appear insignificant and tiny. In the festive and almost feverish excitement of the scene,

> Jason and Sara themselves are standing there, standing under the burning sun near the first shed, giving over their own load, watching their own tomatoes shoved into the process, swallowed away—sorted, wrapped, loaded, dispatched in a freight car—all so fast. . . . Mr. Perkins holds out his hard, quick hand. Shake it fast! How quickly it is all over! (115)

The existence of the Mortons and sharecroppers are rendered insignificant and isolated in productive seasons as well as in harsh seasons. Even the ripe season only gives them a vision that is too "fleeting" according to Marrs' interpretation (24). The brief warmth only results in accentuating the devastation that they will have to endure after the transient season is over.

Porter also treats the theme of Southern poverty in several short stories such as "He" and "Noon Wine." In "He," the author portrays the harshness of rural poverty by depicting the hard life of a mentally retarded person and his poor family. Like the Mortons in "The Whistle" by Welty, the Whipple family in "He" by Porter are poverty-stricken sharecroppers in the rural South. The second child of the Whipple family is mentally retarded, called simply "He" throughout the story. In "The Whistle" by Welty, readers discern the permeating theme of isolation as a major psychological adversity into which the Mortons have been placed as the result of poverty. Similarly, in "He" by Porter, we observe a conspicuous pattern of isolation. As in many other stories discussed so far, the story includes at least several layers of isolation, but the most prominent of all the intertwining conditions of isolation in "He" is the Whipples' isolated position in the community of their neighborhood. Very little, virtually nothing, is told about the circumstance of their neighbors. Readers suppose, however, that they are also poverty-stricken sharecroppers like the Whipples. What separates the Whipples from at least their immediate neighbors is that one of their children is mentally retarded, a circumstance which the neighbors do not share. Mrs. and Mr. Whipple are doubly burdened because of the child's retardation compared with their neighbors who also probably suffer at least from poverty. Throughout the story, readers keep hearing the buzzy gossip-like talk of their neighbors. The neighbors do two things. They blame the parents, Mrs. and Mr. Whipple, for how He was born and how He is. Secondly, they blame the parents for what the parents make him do, because Mr. and Mrs. Whipple make even their retarded child work for their farm and household due to their difficult living conditions. Although it is likely that the neighbors' living conditions are as pressed as those of the Whipples and that they also make every one of their children work, somehow they assume that Mr. and Mrs. Whipple should not make the retarded child work.

A large part of the story is told from the viewpoint of Mrs. Whipple, which has made it possible for many critics to think that Mrs. Whipple is proud, vain, and overly self-conscious and to take her proud disposition as the cause for her being constantly annoyed by what the neighbors say about her and her husband. These critics say that Mrs. Whipple does not love the retarded child so much as she is terribly concerned about what others think of her as a mother. At several points in the story, readers see Mrs. Whipple being driven crazy by the situation and by what others might think of and say about her and her husband. If what many critics say about Mrs. Whipple's personality and problem is true, one might say that Mrs. Whipple drives herself crazy. However, although much of the story is told from her viewpoint, at one point in the story, close to the beginning section, the author clearly interposes a third-party unmitigated observation of the neighbors' conduct, of how they talk about the Whipples behind their backs. Mrs. Whipple desperately tries to do her best to face the difficult circumstance and to act lovingly toward the retarded child, and tells people how much she loves Him for fear that they might think that she does not love him. It is told that all that the Whipples do on their part does not stop the neighbors from talking about them.

> This didn't keep the neighbors from talking plainly among themselves. "A Lord's pure mercy if He should die," they said. "It's the sins of the fathers," they agreed among themselves. "There's bad blood and bad doings somewhere, you can bet on that." This behind the Whipple's backs. To their faces everybody said, "He's not so bad off. He'll be all right yet. Look how He grows!" (*Flowering Judas* 62)

The unsympathetic attitude of the neighbors may not have resulted from mean intentions. However, their lack of insight, sensitivity, and imagination has led them to act the way they do.

"It's the neighbors," says Mrs. Whipple to Mr. Whipple (64). "Oh, I do mortally wish they would keep out of our business" (64). She is afraid that "they'll come nosing around about" what they make Him do on the farm and in the household (64). She also says, "I get sick of people coming around saying things all the time" (65). Readers observe the most serious instance of Mrs. Whipple's desperation about being talked about in one of the moments in the story when she is most pathetic in worrying about the danger that might befall

Him. One day she makes Him take a bull home. While she waits for Him to come back with it, she begins to be frantically worried about the possible danger of Him being suddenly gored by the creature. The thought of a possible accident becomes utterly unbearable for Mrs. Whipple. When He finally appears on a lane where she can see Him from the house, she cannot stand it any longer and begins to scream to admonish Him. He does not seem to hear her, and the bull continues to follow Him calmly. Mrs. Whipple's tension reaches the highest at this point.

> Mrs. Whipple stopped calling and ran towards the house, praying under her breath: "Lord, don't let anything happen to Him. Lord, you *know* people will say we oughtn't to have sent Him. You *know* they'll say we didn't take care of Him. Oh, get Him home, safe home, safe home, and I'll look out for Him better! Amen." (72-73)

As she watches Him lead the bull into the barn, she entirely discards any pretense, feeling that the whole situation is utterly unbearable and being on the verge of nervous breakdown. "She sat down and rocked and cried with her apron over her head" (73). It is startling that in this instance of her utmost desperation when she takes her final recourse of screaming in a prayer, she repeatedly alludes to what the neighbors might say if anything happens to Him. The author emphasizes both allusions in italics, "you *know* they'll say . . ." (73). Although the author has no religious intention in making Mrs. Whipple pray at this moment in the story, her frantic prayer reveals how deep-rooted her worry over others' comments is in her consciousness.

Such an observation of her consciousness has led many critics to view Mrs. Whipple as vain. However, the situation of the Whipples from yet another viewpoint, another possible interpretation, is that the nosy, inconsiderate neighbors have unnecessarily interfered to a large extent with the life of the Whipples without offering them a helping hand, and that their unsympathetic remarks have cut deeply into Mrs. Whipple's psychological wound and trauma. The attitude of the community of the neighbors has triply burdened the Whipples. It has added the third major burden in their life in addition to the burden of poverty and of having a retarded member in the family.

That Mrs. Whipple worries about the comments of the neighbors if anything happens to Him even in her most desperate prayer does not necessarily prove that Mrs. Whipple does not love the retarded child. Just because her frantic prayer incorporates her desperate concern about the neighbors' comments as well as her utmost concern for the child's safety, one cannot conclude that she does not love Him. Her concern about the neighbors' attitude is not necessarily the result of her loving Him less. It does not take away from the extent of her love for Him. Her concern over others' thoughts is simply the result of her being a social being as any other human. In his observation of prevalent critical comments that have criticized Mrs. Whipple for her vanity, Tanner emphasizes the

point that nobody's thought is entirely free of concerns about one's social surroundings because nobody can afford to live in a social vacuum.

The neighbors blame Mrs. and Mr. Whipple for not being caring enough for
Him just because they make him work, but their sentiment about the retarded
child of the Whipple family is *by no means* truly sympathetic. They only blame
the mother and the father for the sake of gossiping. They blame the parents for
not being loving enough toward the child, but on their parts, needless to say,
they do not love the child of the Whipples in the least. As has been quoted, they
say, "A Lord's pure mercy if He should die" (49). The bottom line is that they
do not care. *If* they do at all, it makes no difference because they have not offered any help. Or, they are also so poverty-stricken that nobody can afford to
help anybody in need, although they have enough time and energy left to gossip.
Or, if they help at all, their intention is so imbued with condescension and the
posture of superiority that the recipient of the charity cannot help resist being
pitied and condescended to.

What we observe in the attitude and the words of the neighbors of the
Whipples is the tendency of a community not to accept and cope with a peculiar
predicament of an individual or a family in it. Even when the peculiarity is
slight, a community tends to react like the neighbors to the Whipples. We have
observed a similar phenomenon in the way Mrs. Larkin's neighbors treat Mrs.
Larkin and her adversity in "A Curtain of Green" by Welty. Both Mrs. Whipple
and Mrs. Larkin intensely resist the neighbors' curious and unsympathetic attitudes. Just as Mrs. Larkin cannot stand neighbors' visits which they pay, at best,
out of curiosity and formality, Mrs. Whipple in "He" cannot stand how the
neighbors interfere with her life without genuinely understanding her difficulties. For this reason, Mrs. Whipple feels that she cannot "stand to be pitied" and
that she hates to depend on "charity" (61, 75-76). On the surface, it might seem
that her refusal to rely on charity results from her proud and stubborn disposition. However, the "charity" that can be expected in the kind of community that
buzzes with such comments as quoted above might not be the kind that a suffering family can genuinely appreciate. When Mrs. Whipple says to Mr. Whipple,
"nobody's going to get a chance to look down on us," she may sound proud and
obstinate (61). However, as we observe in the comments of the neighbors in
"He," and in the way Mrs. Larkin's neighbors physically look down on her frantic activities in the garden from the windows above, a community tends to "look
down" on its members in difficulty instead of supporting them. It is usually, or
at least most of the time, unable to regard the peculiar predicament of a certain
individual as part of its own problem and regards the suffering as entirely unrelated to other less suffering members, although, potentially, it is highly probable
any kind of suffering can befall other members any time.

These observations make one question what a human community is. What
is its purpose? A person desires to belong to and to be accepted in a community
so as not to be isolated. However, when even a slight peculiarity of one's circumstance forces one to stray away from a community, or when it fails to support a person or a family during their predicament, the purpose of a community

is blurred. In "He" by Porter and "A Curtain of Green" by Welty, communities appear only as groups for gossiping about others' sufferings, which a group of people lacking consideration, insight, and intellect engage in. The communities in these two stories do not function to prevent one from being isolated. To the contrary, they do isolate the protagonists. In "He," the community of the neighbors isolates the Whipples and drives Mrs. Whipple crazy.

Readers observe another layer of isolation of the Whipples in their problematic relationships with their relatives. When Mrs. Whipple's brother's family visits them, Mrs. Whipple insists that they butcher one of their baby pigs, although Mr. Whipple insists that it would be too much sacrifice for them in their present poor living conditions. Mrs. Whipple retorts, "It's a shame and a pity we can't have a decent meal's vittle once in a while when my own family comes to see us" (65). Again, readers see how much Mrs. Whipple is concerned about what others say about them: "I'd hate for his wife to go back and say there wasn't a thing in the house to eat," and insists that they spend money where they should (65). Again such remarks on her part make it possible to think that Mrs. Whipple is vain and is preoccupied by appearances. However, it is quite possible to infer, from the conduct of the neighbors observed so far, what attitude the brother's family have and what they say about the Whipples away from the town where the Whipples live. Although one might assume that the brother and his family should be closer to the Whipples, and more understanding and compassionate than the neighbors because of the difficult situation of the Whipples, they are not necessarily so. The brother and his family live in a town geographically distant from where the Whipples live, and do not get to see much of what actually goes on in the difficult life of the Whipple family. Psychologically the brother and his family are no more understanding and compassionate than the neighbors, and lend no more actual help to the Whipples. When Mrs. Whipple is afraid that the brother's wife might "go back and say there wasn't a thing in the house to eat," it is quite possible to infer that the brother's wife does make comments of this sort "behind the Whipple's backs" just as the neighbors do (62, 65).

When the brother's family comes, readers see that they are far better off than the Whipples: "The brother came with his plump healthy wife and two great roaring hungry boys" (67). After they have "a grand dinner," which the Whipples have prepared by stretching themselves to the utmost extent despite their sheer poverty, the brother casually and unintentionally drops a comment: "This looks like prosperity all right" (67). The economic gap between the Whipples and the family of the brother is so great that when the Whipples stretch themselves most, they barely reach the standard of the level of affluence that the brother's family considers "all right." Having managed to put up the show of decent affluence and happiness in front of the brother's family, Mrs. Whipple feels temporarily happy and suggests something more extravagant than what they have barely managed to offer: "Oh, we've got six more of these; I say it's as little as we can do when you come to see us so seldom" (68). Because

Mrs. Whipple desperately tries to put up the appearance of decent affluence, the Whipples end up managing to appear not too poor, and the brother's family goes back to their town without realizing how poverty-stricken the Whipples are. If the brother's family never get to know the actual difficulty of the Whipples, it is entirely unlikely that they think about offering them any help. In this sense, it is possible to believe that Mrs. Whipple might be sacrificing help that they might get from their relatives by desperately keeping up appearances.

Why is Mrs. Whipple, then, so anxious to keep up appearances in front of the relatives as well as the neighbors? The first reason she does all this is that, as can be inferred from (1) a comment by the brother that "this looks like prosperity all right," (2) Mrs. Whipple's fears of what the brother's wife might say, and (3) the neighbors' conduct, that it is only likely that the relatives also, at best, talk about the difficulty of the Whipples without offering any help. In the worst case, even the relations are also quite likely to blame them like the neighbors.

The second reason why Mrs. Whipple desperately keeps up appearances is because, like Jason and Sara Morton in "The Whistle" by Welty, at times, Mrs. Whipple becomes awfully tempted to immerse herself in an illusion of being affluent. When the brother drops a comment that the Whipples seems to be doing "all right" and makes a joke about it, saying, "you're going to have to roll me home like I was a barrel when I'm done," Mrs. Whipple temporarily becomes so happy. "Everybody laughed out loud; it was fine to hear them laughing all at once around the table. Mrs. Whipple felt warm and good about it" (67-68). It is at this point that she brags about six more sucking pigs and encourages more visits by the brother's family, which is nothing but the stretching of an illusion on the part of Mrs. Whipple.

However, just as Sara Morton's illusion of the shipping of the cargoes full of tomatoes in the summer and Jason Morton's attempt to kindle up a sudden burst of fire by burning furniture, Mrs. Whipple's illusion of prosperity only leads her, a moment later, to a worse desperation in face of their reality. Just as burning furniture leaves Jason and Sara Morton even more destitute than before, consuming their baby pig has only left the Whipples more economically strained than before. During the dinner and shortly after the brother's family has left, Mrs. Whipple keeps thinking that the brother's family is so nice and decent because they do not make any annoying remarks about the retarded son and the way they treat Him. This is another form of Mrs. Whipple's wishful thinking, and it is also shattered too soon by the sarcastic and doubting, but realistic comment of Mr. Whipple. When Mrs. Whipple says, "That's the way my whole family is. Nice and considerate about everything. No out-of-the-way remarks— they *have* got refinement. I get awfully sick of people's remarks. Wasn't that pig good?" Mr. Whipple replies, "Yes, we're out three hundred pounds of pork, that's all. It's easy to be polite when you come to eat. Who knows what they had in their minds all along" (69). His comment suddenly flings Mrs. Whipple back to her usual neurotic preoccupation with what others say about how the Whipples treat their retarded son. She says angrily to Mr. Whipple, "I don't expect anything else from you. You'll be telling me next that my own brother will be saying around that we made Him eat in the kitchen!" (69). She exclaims, "Oh, my God!" shaking "her head in her hands," because "a hard pain started in the very middle of her forehead" (69). She cannot help continuing to pour out her desperate feeling, while constantly being worried about what the brother's family might say about how they treat the retarded son: "it's all spoiled, and everything was so nice and easy. All right, you don't like them and you never did—all right, they'll not come here again soon, never you mind! But they *can't* say He wasn't dressed every lick as good as Adna—oh, honest, sometimes I wish I was dead!" (69). Mr. Whipple becomes tired of what Mrs. Whipple keeps saying, and says, "I wish you'd let up" (69). However, his next, last remark that day about their own situation sums up everything about them, "It's bad enough as it is" (69).

As the last particular remark of Mrs. Whipple in the middle of the story sums up, the story of "He" by Porter is more about the poverty-stricken family, who are otherwise totally normal and ordinary people, in the context of the Southern exploitive system of sharecropping than it is about Mrs. Whipple's vanity and her failure to love their retarded child. Tanner puts it plainly: "In other words, the Whipples are people just like us. That is the true horror of this story properly contemplated" (Tanner 105). Tanner quotes Emmons in discussing the relation between the character of the Whipples and the hard condition they are placed in: "Inherently they are neither virtuous nor vicious, nor are they any more contemptible than any other people are when bereft of civilizing influences" (Tanner 104, Emmons 28). Tanner draws readers' attention to the social context of the Whipples rather than to moralistic but common critical judgments on the inherent vice or virtue of the Whipple family: "What practically all critics of this story have failed to bring into proper focus is the hard-scrabble existence of sharecropping Texas farmers.[4] This social and economic context, the same, essentially, as that faced by the Thompsons of "Noon Wine," makes moralistic judgments irrelevant" (Tanner 103-04). Viewing and observing the comments and attitude of the neighboring community and possible comments and attitude of others that surround the Whipples, including Mrs. Whipple's brother's family, from this social, holistic viewpoint, the moralistic judgments of those that surround the Whipples are irrelevant just as the judgments of critics are. Viewed through the present interpretation, "He" is not so much about the failure of a particular family and an individual mother to love a retarded child or the failure of the Whipples to properly and openly reach out to each other and the community for help instead of isolating themselves due to their pride as it is about the failure on the part of the community, i.e., a society, to relate meaningfully and relevantly to the suffering of one of its members and to function as a wholesome community. It is too optimistic to assume that the failure is on the part of Mrs. Whipple, because that optimism is based on the unrealistic assumption that the community of the neighbors would be more sympathetic, helpful, and less gossipy *if only* the Whipple family properly loved their retarded son, were less proud, and reached out more openly to others in the community instead of isolating themselves. The Whipple family does love their retarded son within the harsh constraints in which they are placed, and they are not inherently more proud than anybody else. The argument might seem like that of the egg and the chicken, i.e., which was first, Mrs. Whipple's being stubborn, proud, and neurotic and isolating herself and her family from the community, or, the community's talking about, blaming, and segregating the family with a retarded child? Which was first, the Whipples' isolating themselves or the community's isolating them? Either way, criticizing Mrs. Whipple or the community, critical comments might not escape being judgmental. The neighbors, who might also be as poverty-stricken as the Whipples, might not be able to possibly afford to offer any help or money to the Whipples. Judging the community might be as irrelevant as judging the Whipples, considering the possible poverty of the neighbors. However, the question still definitely remains: Need the neighbors gossip and blame the Whipples in the way they do, if they cannot afford to offer any actual help? As a counter-, and balancing argument to criticisms of Mrs. Whipple as a vain person lacking in genuine love for the retarded son, one thing is clear; if one may point out that Porter's piercing skepticism, richness, and complexity as a writer enabled her to undermine the orthodox notion of the love of a mother (Brinkmeyer 102), one can also point out that the very same assets of the author, i.e., Porter's unrelenting skepticism, richness and capacity for complexity as a writer, made her relentlessly reveal the failure of a society as well; that is, the harsh, unsympathetic attitude of the community that surrounds the suffering family. The observation of a similar failure of society in "A Curtain of Green" by Welty strengthens this particular direction of interpretation.

Kate Chopin also wrote stories on a major social issue of the American South in the period, that is, on the issue of racism and how it isolates individuals in society. In "Désirée's Baby" and "La Belle Zoraïde" she writes on the harsh treatment of the female protagonists by white people around them. Both Désirée and Zoraïde live lives of materialistic luxury as dainty ladies. Désirée has been raised by Madame Valmondé, who had picked up Désirée at her toddling age, when she was left at the gateway of Valmondé, possibly by a party of Texans traveling in a canvas-covered wagon (240). Childless Madame Valmondé decides to raise the toddler as her own child. Eighteen years later, Armand Aubigny, the proud son of the rich Aubigny family, falls passionately in love with Désirée, and, without any second thought, immediately proposes to her. As a treasured adopted child of the Valmondés and as an adored, newlywed wife of the prestigious Aubigny family, Désirée lives a life as a fine, fair, dainty lady, up until a certain point. Zoraïde, with skin the "color of *café-au-lait*" and some black blood, serves Madame Delariviere, but her position is such that she never has been ordered to do any "rougher work than sewing a fine muslin seam" and is given "her own little black servant to wait upon her" (304). Madame Delariviere, her mistress, is also her godmother, and takes extra trouble seeing to what she calls the "honor to your bringing up" (304). Thus, Zoraïde lives a life of luxury for some time as an envied, "elegant," "graceful" lady, always the object of "the envy" (304). With both Désirée and Zoraïde, people around them consider their beauty as their major asset, and up to a certain point, their luxurious mode of living seems to assure the happiness that their beauty has bought. However, very soon, their happiness tumbles away rather tragically. It is soon revealed that the happiness and luxury earned through their grace are not solid. In the kind of way of life in which their beauty and elegance are considered their major assets, they are treated by the people who rule their lives as only things and ornaments, but not as individuals with their own initiative. In both "Désirée's Baby" and "La Belle Zoraïde," the problem of the extreme lack of control that the beautiful, feminine protagonists have over their own lives is also the issue of female subjugation. However, in both stories, their predicaments as subjugated females are aggravated by the problem of racism that labels them as belonging to an inferior race. Ellen Peel repeatedly emphasizes in "Semiotic Subversion in 'Désirée's Baby'" that the story involves three layers of subversion, by race, sex, and class. Zoraïde in "La Belle Zoraïde" also suffers from these three layers of subjugation.

Especially in "Désirée's Baby" the issue of racism is a complex, dominant theme because the ending of the story leaves readers to imagine a number of possibilities as to the lives of Désirée and Armand Aubigny. Their lives are ruled and tossed by racism, and they are totally isolated from each other in the end. Although it is not entirely impossible to interpret Désirée's tragedy as more of an individualistic nature caused by Armand Aubigny's idiosyncratic vices than caused by racism, the issue of racism is a central theme of the story. To attribute the cause of the tragedy solely or chiefly to characters' individual traits or peculiarities of a circumstance is to blur and evade the central social issue. Peel refers to the approach to the story by Cynthia Griffin Wolff, who emphasizes the story's personal and interior approach, and who comments that the racism is ultimately "emblematic." In Wolff's view, the ironic and unstated fact is that "human situations can *never* be as clear as 'black and white' " (Wolff 127-28). While admitting Wolff's point to some extent, Peel maintains that the issue of race has a literal function as well as an "emblematic meaning" (Peel 71). Just as Peel stressed the literal function of race, sex, and class, it shall be *re*-emphasized that the fact that human conditions can never be analyzed through clear-cut dichotomy, for instance, of "black and white," does not erase the seriousness of and the necessity of recognizing existing social issues of whatever types of segregation in a society.

Simply, Kate Chopin's subtle and sensitive artistry as an author enabled her to add enough personal and internal tones while developing a plot centering on racism. While treating a serious social issue, Chopin managed to avoid making the story have only dichotomous dimensions and sound like moral preaching or what Welty regards as agitating propagandas. However, with authors like Chopin, Welty, and Porter, who all treated major social issues in some of their stories, their personal, interior, and psychological approaches do *not* make the social issues any more vague. Approaches that emphasize the personal, psychological impact of circumstances on characters are by no means incompatible with effective depiction of social problems. Rather, especially in cases of stories like "Désirée's Baby" and "La Belle Zoraïde" by Chopin, Chopin's ability to give a personal and interior touch to the plot dealing with racism accentuates and intensifies, rather than dims, the devastating effect of racism on the lives of individuals. As Welty repeatedly stresses in "Must the Novelist Crusade?", writings of the types of "inflammatory tracts" often fail to delve into the true seriousness of individual cases. Consequently they betray their original purpose to appeal for the suffering people. To the contrary, successful literature, which does not fail to give a "personal and interior," and sometimes, an "emblematic," touch to whatever subject it deals with can be more effective than "inflammatory tracts" for the purposes of the latter. In analyzing successful literature that treats major social issues, it is up to readers and critics not to miss the significance of the treated social issues even if the approach is "personal and interior." To dispute whether a story's approach is personal and interior, or centered on a social issue is, again, to argue about a chicken and an egg. To dispute which are to be blamed, individuals, or a social system, is only to take away responsibility from either of them, and in the case of the discussion of literature, is only to narrow the wide scope that a writer was able to create due to her artistic and literary talent. In discussing "Désirée's Baby" by Chopin, one does not give a just treatment to it if one discerns only, on one hand, individual traits such as Armand Aubigny's tyrannical disposition and Désirée's passivity, or, on the other hand, racism.

In "Désirée's Baby" the characterization of Armand Aubigny by the author is to make him symbolize the racist social stratum, although some, for instance, the other characters in the story, may think that the circumstance may not have been so bad had it not been for Armand's cold, rigid disposition, and some may not fully admit the seriousness of the discriminatory social stratum of the period as an ultimate cause of their unhappiness. Peel observes that Désirée and other characters seem to feel that the cause of their miserable situation is the personal idiosyncrasy of Armand, such as his lack of pity and sympathy, and that they do not seem to recognize the institutional nature of exploitation based on race, class, and sex (Peel 71). Chopin characterizes Armand Aubigny so that one kind of the worst consequences of racism is concentrated in him. Through the characterization of Armand Aubigny, who is by no means portrayed favorably, the author makes "Désirée's Baby" an indictment of racism.

Already earlier in the story, before the plot develops to reveal that the baby born to Désirée and Armand has some black blood, and before Armand begins to act cruelly to Désirée, readers discern the foreshadowing of the tragedy in the characterization of Armand and the description of the mansion of the Aubignys. In the early stage of the story, in terms of the Désirée-Armand lovers' plot, Désirée and Armand are at the height of their happiness as a newly-wed couple, being intoxicated with each other and having just had a new-born baby whose black blood nobody has yet discerned. However, the shadow is already definitely there. When Madame Valmondé comes to L'Abri, the mansion of the proud Aubigny family, to see the new-born baby of Désirée and Armand, as a foster mother of Désirée, already, just its sight depressed her, although the occasion is supposedly the happy one of visiting a new-born baby of her newly-wed adopted daughter. The presented imagery already suggests much terror.

> When she reached L'Abri she shuddered at the first sight of it, as she always did. It was a sad looking place, which for many years had not known the gentle presence of a mistress, old Monsieur Aubigny having married and buried his wife in France, and she having loved her own land too well ever to leave it. The roof came down steep and black like a cowl, reaching out beyond the wide galleries that encircled the yellow stuccoed house. Big solemn oaks grew close to it, and their thick-leaved, far-reaching branches shadowed it like a pall. Young Aubigny's rule was a strict one, too, and under it his negroes had forgotten how to be gay, as they had been during the old master's easy-going and indulgent lifetime. (241)

Since the plot of the tragedy does not yet quite unfold at this point of the story, the dark imagery of L'Abri and the dark side of Armand's disposition might seem to have been presented only to accentuate, through contrast, the torrid happiness that the lightening of youthful passion between Désirée and Armand has brought to them. Hopefully, the passion of proud Armand for Désirée and Désirée's exquisite beauty and tender disposition work as magic and completely cast away the dark curse of L'Abri and its young, but cruel master. If the tale develops in such a happy direction, the cloud of evil that envelops L'Abri simply accentuates the power and wonder of amorous passion, youthful female beauty, and the sweetness of docile, feminine disposition, which have power to dispel even the adamant curse. The story would be a happy-ending fairy tale for both Armand Aubigny and Désirée. Désirée, who was deserted by a party of traveling Texans in her early childhood and had no family, is to become the adored, young wife of the son of the wealthy, prestigious, prominent family of the area thanks to Armand's passion for her. The cruel, dark disposition of Armand Aubigny will be completely thawed and transformed thanks to the passion between him and Désirée. Cinderella is discovered by a rich prince, and a fierce frog in the dark marsh will be transformed into a gentle prince. Of course, Chopin's realism and capacity as a writer to discern the existing social problem of the period do not allow such a development. The gloom of L'Abri is not merely a background that contrasts with a happy development, nor is Armand Aubigny's disposition to be transformed only to accentuate a happy transformation. Rather, the darkness of L'Abri presented in the beginning is the foundation of the entire plot, and the cruelty of Armand Aubigny, the permeating base of the whole story. They do not change. Rather, they become worse after having gone through an extremely transient phase of softening and warming.

Even during the temporary phase when their "marriage and the birth of their son had softened Armand Aubigny's imperious and exacting nature greatly," readers continue to see the insistent pattern in him that is soon to develop into the stormy burst of his vice, that is, his adamant preoccupation with his "name" that is symbolic of rigid class and race divisions (242). In the beginning of the plot even when he is suddenly seized by the burst of blind passion, his reason for not caring a straw about Désirée's obscure origin is sustained by his rigid belief in the value of the class and race to which he believes he belongs. His passion and Désirée's qualities have not entirely transformed him, if one observes carefully. That is, they have not entirely overthrown the basic value system of race and class segregation on which Armand Aubigny bases his entire being and life. When Monsieur Valmondé, the foster father of Désirée, became apprehensive because of Désirée's "obscure origin" and honestly told him that "she was nameless," it is narrated that Armand did not heed, being swept away by passion (241). However, at the bottom of his feelings is the thought of his name: "What did it matter about a name when he could give her one of the oldest and proudest in Louisiana?" (241). Even in the midst of her happiness, Désirée is also aware of Armand's strong self-consciousness of his name and class. She says, and this is in the peak of her happiness, "Oh, Armand is the proudest father in the parish, I believe, chiefly because it is a boy, to bear his name; though he says not–that he would have loved a girl as well. But I know it isn't true. I know he says that to please me" (242). Although Désirée well discerns Armand's pride of his family name and his strong belief that the name shall be continued through the birth of his offspring, at this point, she does not discern that he builds his pride by rigidly segregating those who do not belong to what he believes to be his own class and race and that he is also a strong sexist in believing only in male lineage. Soon the plot builds up to reveal that the three-month-old son between them has some black blood, and the great harm that can be brought about by Armand's strong consciousness and pride of his name fully emerges. Désirée and the readers are struck by his change, although it is not a change, but only the emergence of his basic nature and the disappearance of a temporary happiness: "he no longer loved her, because of the unconscious injury she had brought upon his home and his name" (244). As Peel points out, when Armand begins to condemn and curse Désirée, Désirée is so entirely passive and in a vulnerable position that it does not even occur to her to protest, or to suggest that the black blood might be on his side, or from both of them, but not solely from her side (70). Similarly, on the part of Armand, his confidence in what he believes of his class and race is so strong that the possibility of black blood on his side never occurs to him and he stormily condemns Désirée. The dark, cursed imagery of a racist social stratum that the author already establishes in the beginning of the story through the depiction of the gloom of L'Abri and the characterization of Armand Aubigny culminates in the wicked mood and behavior of Armand toward Désirée and others after the disclosure. His treatment of the slaves reverts to its former, cruel manner. Rather, it becomes worse than ever: "the very spirit of Satan seemed suddenly to take hold of him in his dealings with the slaves" (242). He acts extremely coldly toward Désirée and feels like hurting her as much as possible: "He thought Almighty God had dealt cruelly and unjustly with him; and felt, somehow, that he was paying Him back in kind when he stabbed thus into his wife's soul" (244). When Désirée finally decides to disappear from L'Abri, she shows him the brief letter from her foster mother, Madame Valmondé, that tells Désirée to come back to Valmondé. Désirée asks him, "Shall I go, Armand?" "in tones sharp with agonized suspense" (243). His answers are extremely curt, sharp, and cold. "Yes, go." "Do you want me to go?" "Yes, I want you to go" (243). When Désirée finally walks away, still somewhat "hoping he would call her back," she utters in anguish, "Good-by, Armand," to which he does not answer, because he feels that acting in such a way towards his wife "was his last blow at fate" (244). The imagery Chopin uses to depict Armand Aubigny's extremely harsh racism which is not even grounded on a confirmed truth of his own entire whiteness is that of Lucifer rebelling against God and Fate, although it is by no means Chopin's intention to give a moral or religious sermon. The imagery of one of the extreme instances of racism culminates in Armand Aubigny's ruling over the sight of a burning fire, arousing the imagery of hell fire.

> Some weeks later there was a curious scene enacted at L'Abri. In the centre of the smoothly swept back yard was a great bonfire. Armand Aubigny sat in the wide hallway that commanded a view of the spectacle; and it was he who dealt out to a half dozen negroes the material which kept this fire ablaze. (244)

The materials of the bonfire are all of Désirée and the baby's belongings such as the exquisite wedding *corbeille*, her delicate, dainty clothing, the baby's cradle of an exceptional making, and lastly, the packet of "innocent," short letters Désirée had sent him during their engagement (244). If Désirée kills herself and the baby after her disappearance from L'Abri, which is certainly one of the possible interpretations of her life afterwards and which many readers take, Armand figuratively burns Désirée and the baby in the fire as well as their belongings, an act comparable to some instances of burning of a bride in India when the dowry is not enough: Désirée and the baby are not good enough for the Aubigny family.

Of course, as Peel discusses, Désirée may not kill herself and the baby. In some readers' opinions, she does not need to kill herself just because she is deserted by Armand and Aubigny family. As Peel mentions, she may rather emancipate herself from being confined for the rest of her life in the rigidity and coldness of the much too proud family by disappearing from L'Abri (Peel 68). If she kills herself and the baby, however, she conforms to the value system of segregation of Armand Aubigny in destroying herself and baby whose blood she, also possibly wrongly, believes, deviates from the valued blood in that particular system. Is it not too possible for her to hate and rebel against a man like Armand Aubigny, especially if she completely disappears from L'Abri never to return, which is actually what she does, and never has to have anything to do with Armand and other members of Aubigny family, and start a completely new life, although she may have to struggle greatly to do so? She only needs to give up living in an extraordinarily spacious mansion, being served by many slaves, wearing dainty clothing of exceptional materials, and being adored by a man whose nature is inherently not so generous and open, all of which to modern readers seem not significant enough to mourn the loss of, let alone to kill oneself for. However, the ultimate terror and danger of a discriminatory social stratum is that once a person is placed in a certain higher rank in the stratum, it becomes extremely hard, almost impossible, for the person to grow out of the value system. Edith Wharton develops a similar plot in *The House of Mirth,* in which it becomes extremely difficult for the female protagonist, Lily Bart, to give up the luxurious, dainty mode of living once she is used to it and to get out of the corrupted moneyed society in order to regain spiritual and moral freedom and purity. She also ends up killing herself. It becomes impossible for a fly to get out of an open bottle once it is in it, although to outside, objective observers, it is only its folly not to be able to see that the exit is completely open. Unless Désirée finds out, by some chance, that Armand has black blood, even if she does not kill herself, she might keep living in misery, cursing herself for the blood branded inferior. If that is the consequence, the greater harm that Armand does to her in deserting her is in his having destroyed her inherent self-esteem as an individual than in the deserting itself.

So far in the plot, Armand is portrayed as an active agent of the vice of racism, and Désirée, as its victim. However, the plot and the crux of the theme of racism are not entirely developed until the very end of the story. There is the famous twist at the end. When Armand puts a bundle of letters by Désirée in the bonfire, he discovers an old letter in the back of the drawer that is not by Désirée. The letter is from his deceased mother to his father, in which she is grateful to God that their son, Armand, is not to know that his mother has black blood. Although the Désirée-plot is certainly tragic because she is victimized, the final Armand Aubigny-plot is even more complex and darker. All the destructive elements of his racism are to feed back upon himself. The effects of self-destruction and self-hatred can be more dangerous, complex, and more destructive than destroying others. On one hand, Armand has a choice to continue to conceal the origin of his birth and to live and act as a master and a white man. However, having already found out the truth, it will be psychologically extremely complex for him to continue to live a life of concealing the truth. Chopin lets the dark, gloomy imagery of L'Abri and the Satanic imagery of Armand Aubigny take the darkest path, the path that very possibly leads to psychological self-destruction, the most dangerous type of isolation. Any type of social segregation is always prone to the possibility of self-destruction because of the inherent potential possibility for any established stratum to be reversed any time. A mentality that segregates others is highly prone to self-destruction because it confines and isolates itself in a hard core and shuts away interactions with others different from itself, and thus hampers its own growth. A mentality prone to segregate others is inherently highly susceptible to self-destruction because it segregates others because of its own deep-rooted mental insecurity. In segregating others, it tries to build walls to protect its vulnerable self-esteem, but in doing so, its insecurity grows worse and worse because, in building walls for discriminating against others, it grows more and more paranoid about maintaining the hard shell that camouflages its insecurity, and thereby builds up insecurity rather than curing it.

Readers observe an inseparable, severe relationship between self-destruction and isolation within a community, i.e., the lack of meaningful relationships to others, in *The Awakening* as well as in "Désirée's Baby." Although it is quite obvious that Edna is an isolated individual in a Creole community, more serious and fatal than her isolated situation itself is her lack of mental energy to seek any type of meaningful solidarity either within or outside the community.[5] Although Edna feels utterly isolated in the community, the community does not ostracize her, because most of her attempts at various forms of self-emancipation are not so revolutionary nor vitally innovative enough to overthrow any aspect of the status quo and to cause a fatally strong opposition of the community. The point is that Edna ostracizes herself before attempting anything that is vital and significant enough to cause the family and society to ostracize her. Although she is not ostracized by society, she grows *fatally* dissatisfied. The way she has played it seems moderate in that she did not cause herself to be criticized too harshly and to be subsequently destroyed by others and a society. Nevertheless, the moderateness, or the feebleness, of her attempts leads her to severe, incurable dissatisfaction that results in self-destruction.

Both for Edna in *The Awakening* and Désirée in "Désirée's Baby" by Chopin, self-destruction, or possible self-destruction, is caused by their complete lack of political awareness, which could have caused them to *seek* some solidarity with anybody or anywhere else.[6] In this sense, they are both extremely isolated protagonists. Edna, bravely to some extent, makes various attempts, but they remain only at a purely inward, individual level, and thus, are rendered quite minor. Désirée does not even make an attempt. Both in *The Awakening* and "Désirée's Baby," readers observe prototypical forms of the most destructive danger in the type of isolation that is caused by lack of political awareness and lack of attempts at forming any solidarity. For Désirée, it may not be an ultimate tragedy to have been deserted by Armand Aubigny. Her real tragedy lies in her failure to discern the political aspect, i.e., racism, of the situation in which she is placed, and her consequent blame of herself and her failure to ever question the political deficiency of the area she lives in, i.e., of the American South.

Notes

1. Jane Robbins Taylor discusses "The Whistle" in her dissertation, *The Rural Poor Whites in Selected Literature of Mississippi Writers*. She observes that among all thirty-nine stories by Welty in her four collections of short stories, three stories are about the rural poor white: "The Whistle," "Death of a Traveling Salesman," and "The Wide Net" (Taylor 12). Taylor analyzes "The Whistle," treating it as a part of Mississippi literature that features the poor white. Taylor considers the theme of the poor white as less explored in literature than the themes of other social classes such as Cajuns, African-Americans, mountaineers, and migrant workers, which she observes have been extensively explored

in literature (Taylor 43). Taylor's dissertation is among the few critical works that have paid serious attention to "The Whistle," which has not received much serious critical attention, having been considered an inferior work among Welty's stories.

However, as is referred to in this chapter, Suzanne Marrs also discusses "The Whistle" in her book, *One Writer's Imagination: The Fiction of Eudora Welty*, and points to the isolation of the couple even from each other.

Naoko Fuwa Thornton also gives her opinion about works by Welty that openly treat social issues, listing "The Whistle" as one of the few stories by Welty that directly deal with social problems. She also includes "Flowers for Marjorie" in this category, while discussing "Where is the Voice Coming From?" and "The Demonstrators" as significantly social, yet neglected works (Thornton, *Strange Felicity* 167). As is treated in Chapter 3 and Chapter 4, this book discusses "Flowers for Marjorie" primarily from the perspectives of family problems and women's issues.

2. Paul E. Mertz observes that landless farmers, mostly share tenants and sharecroppers, were among the most prominent figures in the American South from the post-Civil War years until about the mid-20th century. Sharecroppers were especially subject to exploitive and paternalistic crop-lien tenancy. Southern tenancy represented rural poverty in the American South. In these years the exploitation was built into the tenancy system, which Mertz states was perhaps the greatest tragedy of the system. Planters were in a position to settle whatever exploitive arrangements without being challenged by poor, illiterate tenants (Mertz 29-31).

3. It has been noted that Welty has mentioned a possible source of the composition of "The Whistle." Louise Westling pays special attention to the experience that Welty had when she visited a friend in the country. Late one night during that particular visit, Welty was wakened by a shrill whistle. Her friend explained to Welty about the custom of the landlord in the region of blowing a whistle at night to warn his country people of the freeze that could damage the tomato plants. The sharecroppers were expected to wake up and cover the plants with whatever kinds of covering they could find. In the morning, Welty and her friend saw the consequences. Clothing, bedclothes, and old croker sacks were used all over the field to cover the plants. Referring to what Welty witnessed on that occasion, Westling states that "the shock of such poverty and sacrifice stimulated her to write the story" (Westling 63-64).

4. David E. Conrad observes that the severe lives of the tenant farmers in the South began to draw national attention during the 1930's due to the writings of liberals who depicted the miserable conditions of the southern tenants and proved that poverty existed in America. Conrad mentions John Steinbeck, Erskine Caldwell, James Agee, and Walker Evans (Conrad 1412). Although Katherine Anne Porter and Eudora Welty cannot be classified as socialist writers, their literary capability to depict the harshness of southern poverty and the suffering of people under it as seen in, for instance, "The Whistle" and "He," would let readers maintain that these writers also contributed to drawing public attention to the southern social problem, even if their social influence may not have been as wide as that of other writers mentioned by Conrad.

5. In her discussion of "Désirée's Baby" Ellen Peel emphasizes Désirée's lack of political awareness and her failure to even think about forming any solidarity with others who also have some black blood, for instance, the servants of L'Abri with some black blood (70-71).

6. See note 5.

Chapter 6

Isolation and Writing as Resistance[1]

In the very first line of the classic novel, *Anna Karénina*, Tolstoï wrote, "All happy families resemble one another; every unhappy family is unhappy in its own way" (Tolstoï 1). In this famous first line, the Russian novelist stresses the uniqueness and peculiarities of the sufferings of what he calls "unhappy families." In his words, not one "unhappy family" is like any other "unhappy family," whereas, in his observation, "all happy families" are pretty much alike. Tolstoï does not find any striking uniqueness and peculiarity in the happiness of each "happy family." Using these terms of the Russian novelist about family situations, one may say that, generally, forms and conditions of happiness and welfare are pretty much alike, but that every form and condition of unhappiness is unique and peculiar in its own way.

If this axiomatic beginning of the world-famous novel is true, the statement by Tolstoï may well be the reason for serious novels and stories to have, at least some, or a great number of, "unhappy" developments and elements, because writers are always interested in creating unique experiences in their writings. No serious writer wants to deal with materials that are commonplace and alike. It is also a great test of their talent for ambitious writers to discern unique elements in experiences that appear common and alike in a superficial observation and to bring out the discovered uniqueness to the fullest extent in their writings.

Through the same perception that Tolstoï shows in the beginning of *Anna Karénina*, one can very well say: the states of togetherness resemble one another, whereas every state of isolation is unique and peculiar in its own manner. Since the speckless sense of complete togetherness is based on some sort of illusion most of the time, writers are only truthfully observant and perceptive of human conditions and psychology in discerning patterns of isolation in the experiences of and relationships between the characters in their writings. Once writers detect states of isolation in which characters are placed, their next task is to depict the states of isolation so as to accentuate the uniqueness and peculiarity of each condition of isolation.

What, then, is the purpose of writers in discerning, illustrating, and accentuating the uniqueness of each unhappy family or an isolated individual? Readers might resist the tendency of serious writings to stress unhappy elements and isolated individuals. Do writers seek unhappy, lonely plots only for an art-for-art's-sake pose? Do they use unhappy, lonely plots merely because of their uniqueness and because uniqueness is indispensable for being artistic? Do serious writers and readers regard themselves as superior, deeper, and more artistic simply because they pay attention to darker, unhappy, lonesome aspects of human experiences? Do they think that happiness or togetherness is too shallow and simplistic for their complex, superior minds?

The reason for writers to observe and depict unhappy and isolated circumstances is simply because they aim to be truthful. Eudora Welty repeatedly stresses this point in "Must the Novelist Crusade?" As has been mentioned in Chapter 4, in her terms, fiction writers aim to "show" and "disclose" life as it is, and to "make what's told alive" (Welty 149, 152). If writers succeed in being truthful, as a consequence, they succeed as artists. However, they aspire to be truthful not necessarily for an art-for-art's sake pose. Simply, they know that the blind pursuit and simplistic illustration of happiness and togetherness are usually not free of some falsehood, and misrepresentation is the last element that they want their writings to have. As has been mentioned in Chapter 4, Welty is keenly aware of the danger of the falsehood that writings that are for the purpose of propaganda inherently have and that simplistically attempt to solve and reach a "happy" "solution" right away. Talented writers and insightful thinkers know that a false and forged sense of happiness and togetherness commonly aggravates unhappy feelings and a sense of isolation rather than alleviating them, though they do not necessarily think that unhappiness and loneliness are more sophisticated than and superior to happiness and togetherness. They always attempt to view meaningful forms of happiness and togetherness, when they do at all, rather than depicting seemingly immaculate, but false happiness and togetherness that have been reached through the sacrifice of being false.

Whether or not a writer can relentlessly reveal unhappy situations and isolated psychology instead of creating false hopes depends on the extent of their capability and truthfulness. They are not pessimistic in pursuing truth rather than forged hopes. To the contrary it is not always beneficial to be absolutely certain of solutions, but it can be very harmful to be too self-convinced of reasons and solutions instead of facing and accepting uncertainties and mysteries. In approaching and dealing with problematic and isolated human conditions by truthfully depicting them, writers *accept* them rather than attempt to solve them. Some might condemn such an approach of writers as passive and irresponsible. However, being truthful and accepting need not be equated with being passive and irresponsible. To the contrary, grabbing what one may think of as "solution" or togetherness with self-conviction is possibly less responsible than being truthful in that the approach of the latter type completely disregards necessity and responsibility to face and cope with complex problems, and consequently often simply fails in the end. Eudora Welty's tone is quite defiant in writings whose primary goals do not appear to "solve" or even to "comfort" or "condone" problems and lonely situations of characters. However, need she have been so defiant and defensive if the approach of "inflammatory tracts" is less responsible than that of serious literary writings? *Acceptance* of loneliness on the part of characters and the approach of a writer to truthfully depict their isolation by *accepting* it are not passive attitudes as those who are self-convinced and self-satisfied may think. Rather, *acceptance* is a highly active act, not a passive state, both on the part of characters and writers, that requires the fullest initiative, responsibility, and mental energy.

Miranda in "Old Mortality" by Katherine Anne Porter, discussed in Chapter 4, is the strongest character of all the characters observed so far in this book in her furious will to choose the path of loneliness out of her own active initiative. Her deliberate choice of isolation results from her fierce mental energy that verges on "a fury of jealous possessiveness," as has been observed in Chapter 4 (*Pale Horse* 87). Her will to throw herself relentlessly into isolation is so heedless that it is not without "arrogance" and "ignorance," herself being aware that her probing words about the meaning of life are somewhat "childish" (84, 87, 89). Joan Schulz stresses in "Orphaning as Resistance" that Miranda chooses to make herself "orphaned" (Schulz 93). As Miranda continues her journey and career as a loner in "Pale Horse, Pale Rider," she experiences a new encounter, another process of separation, and an ultimate form of isolation, death. She encounters a new lover, an archetypal American Adam, is separated from him due to his death, and roams between life and death from the flu epidemic.

In many significant major stories by Chopin, Porter, and Welty, the image of death as a final, ultimate form of isolation prevails and dominates. In the stories of the three authors that are best known and most often anthologized, death and isolation are central themes. They are *The Awakening* by Kate Chopin, "Flowering Judas" by Katherine Anne Porter, and "Death of a Traveling Salesman" by Eudora Welty. In each of them, the image of death is a foundation of a plot development and a thematic thread. In all of them, the protagonists face death in some way. In "Flowering Judas" by Porter, Laura enters the world of death in her dream, while being led by her comrade who actually dies from poison that she has carried to him, although Laura herself does not actually die. In "Death of a Traveling Salesman" by Welty, the male protagonist, Bowman, the traveling salesman, dies from a heart problem from which he has been suffering. In *The Awakening*, Edna Pontellier kills herself at the end of the novel. In each of them, the image of death is the direct and ultimate representation of the state of isolation.

In "Flowering Judas," Laura is forced into a realization, through her journey to the threshold of death and life, that her adamant negation of any meaningful human relation and her obstinate encasement of herself in the hard core of isolation have made her live a life of spiritual death. Her comrade, Eugenio, who leaves the world of life for that of the dead by himself entices Laura in her dream to travel with him and shows her how meaningless, deadly, and treacherous her way of life is by condemning her harshly, calling her "Cannibal!" (*Flowering Judas* 160). Although Laura awakens from her dream and comes back to the world of the living by herself, leaving Eugenio to depart to death by himself, spiritually, she only comes back to the life of deathly isolation. In Laura's case, paradoxically, she experiences momentary union with another individual in a dream and death, while continuing to live a life frozen in isolation.

In "Death of a Traveling Salesman," Bowman dies while being literally isolated. Shortly before he dies, he begins to realize that his heart problem is growing worse and worse, and tries to take refuge in a certain house that he spots in the wild openness of the area in which he has been traveling. At that point, his car is stranded in a bush, so he is forced to seek help anyway. At the house he goes to ask to get his car out of the bush, an old woman comes to the door and keeps telling him that she has to wait till a man whom she calls "Sonny" comes back (*A Curtain* 237). When he comes back, he does skillfully pull Bowman's car out of the bush. However, Bowman still feels too sick to travel any farther for the day, and hesitantly asks the old woman and the man if they could let him rest at their place for one night. When they reluctantly consent to Bowman's request, he is suddenly seized by a sense that he is rejected by them, realizing that the woman is not old and that the man is not her son as he has assumed. Bowman finally realizes that they are a young couple and that she is soundly pregnant. He senses that they want to keep out a stranger for fear that their perfect happiness may be intruded upon, and he feels utterly isolated. Although he thinks about staying at their house for that particular night because he feels too sick to be on the road, once he begins to hear their sleeping breath, he leaves the house without seeing them, only leaving some money. Since his heart condition does not quite recover over one night, as soon as he is on the road, his heart begins to beat wildly. Being in sudden acute pain and not wanting anybody to hear his loud heart beats, Bowman presses his chest, but the story closes with the narration that tells, "But nobody heard it" anyway (253). In "Death of a Traveling Salesman" Welty relentlessly makes the theme of isolation lead to the death of the protagonist. The author unflinchingly contrasts the isolated death of the traveling salesman with the expected birth of a baby of the united, young couple by making the couple desert the salesman in his fatal health trouble, or by making the salesman feel that he is rejected by them.

In *The Awakening* by Chopin, Edna Pontellier kills herself, which is the darkest form of death and isolation. Throughout the novel, Edna experiences various patterns of isolation whenever her various aspirations are unfulfilled. She fails to win the respect from and independence from her wealthy, but materialistic, husband. She feels that she finds no spiritual, intellectual, and emotional affinity with him, nor with her children whose welfare is strongly expected by her husband to be ensured at the sacrifice of his wife's spiritual integrity. She fails to be united with her lover, Robert Lebrun, whom she once thought could be a catalyst for her self-emancipation. She continues to feel that she cannot identify with other wives of the Creole community because she fails to find any intellectual stimulus in conversations with them that center on either materialistic or domestic matters. She feels that her attempt to establish her own studio so as to ensure her own time and space does not lead to an ultimate independence because she is not economically independent, which leads her to the sense of ultimate failure.

Especially in the case of Edna Pontellier, her sense that her various aspirations are hampered gives her a sense of meaninglessness. Her feeling that she cannot feel any affinity with others because of their chiefly materialistic interest and that she is isolated in the family and the community aggravates her sense of the meaninglessness of continuing to live at all in such a mode of life. Her sense of isolation does not cause her to *seek* a new place, sphere, and people where and with whom she can unfold and develop her potential. Her sense of failure, sense of meaninglessness, and sense of isolation aggravate each other, and lead to her self-inflicted death.

Perhaps most prototypically in *The Awakening*, but certainly so also in other stories discussed so far, failure, waste, and meaninglessness deeply relate to a sense of isolation for characters, and this sense of isolation causes a sense of death in life in them even if they may not physically die. Within various forms and conditions of isolation observed in previous chapters, readers discern the elements of death. In the stories discussed in "Passion and Isolation," readers see how frustrated and stifled passion symbolizes death at an emotional level. Especially in the stories observed in "Family and Isolation," i.e., "Flowers for Marjorie" and "A Curtain of Green" by Welty and "María Concepción" by Porter, death is at the center of the plots and hovers as a major theme. In "Flowers for Marjorie" and "María Concepción" it culminates in the form of homicide, resulting from isolation and separation of the consciousness of couples between whom hatred has built up. In "A Curtain of Green" death leaves a young widow in isolation. In the stories observed in "Social Issues and Isolation," one sees how poverty renders people spiritually dead and how isolation in a community and lack of comradeship and solidarity can lead to the destruction of individuals comparable to death. Especially in the stories discussed in "Passion and Isolation" and "Family and Isolation," the conditions of isolation are contrasted with the forms of togetherness that individuals and society tend to expect in romantic relationships and in families. The same is true to some extent in the link between isolation of individuals and a ruthless community as has been observed in "Social Issues and Isolation." However, society is a larger unit than individual couples and families, and therefore, potentially can be more resourceful than individual lovers and family members. Certain problems causing isolation and life in death, such as poverty, racism, sexism, and class segregation, seen in the stories treated in other chapters as well as in "Social Issues and Isolation," are sometimes better dealt with by society as a whole than through personal efforts by individuals. Of course, there is the other side of the coin to the larger potential of a community. Once a community begins to run in the direction of being destructive rather than constructive, it can grow totally destructive and literally and psychologically kill excluded and segregated individuals. For instance, in "He" by Porter, the community does not help suffering individuals. In "He" and "Noon Wine" by Porter, "A Curtain of Green" by Welty, "Désirée's Baby" and "La Belle Zoraide" by Chopin, communities exclude individuals with certain peculiar traits or experiences. In "Pale Horse, Pale Rider" and "The Leaning Tower" by Porter, a society enters a dark age of war and fascism and hovers over individuals to shadow their lives.

In the stories discussed in "Feminine Independence and Isolation," the intertwining relationships between isolation, independence and death are much more complex as they are portrayed by Chopin, Porter, and Welty, the prominent women writers of the American South at the turn of the century. Among the female protagonists of the stories treated in the chapter, the ones who actually die are Edna Pontellier in *The Awakening*, Elizabeth Stock in "Elizabeth Stock's One Story," Louise Mallard in "The Story of an Hour" by Chopin, Marjorie in "Flowers for Marjorie" by Welty, María Rosa in "María Concepción," and Ellen Weatherall in "The Jilting of Granny Weatherall" by Porter. It is certainly not possible nor commendable to generalize about the female protagonists who die and who do not die in the stories discussed in the previous chapters. However, one discerns several significant thematic threads concerning isolation, independence, and death of female protagonists. Using the terms that Joan Schulz uses in her article, "Orphaning as Resistance," about stories by women writers centering on female characters in which she mentions Miranda of "Old Mortality," a potential pattern in *The Awakening* is "Death as Resistance." However, one cannot help question whether death was absolutely a sole alternative for Edna to express and enact her resistance. Her death, after all, appears apathetic and self-destructive rather than truly an act of resistance. Has she sufficiently acted out her resistance before she dies so as to make her death have enough impact as "resistance"? If she had done so, her death might have as truly represented "Death as Resistance" as the suicide committed by Mary Pankhurst in England for the specific purpose of winning a right to vote for women. In "Elizabeth Stock's One Story," Elizabeth dies, but possibly more important than her death is her writing, in which she describes her life and the cause of her death and defends herself. The pattern one sees in her "one story" is "Writing as Resistance," although one can hardly be optimistic about what actually befalls Elizabeth.[2] In all these cases, "Orphaning as Resistance" taken by Miranda in "Old Mortality," "Death as Resistance" attempted by Edna Pontellier, and "Writing as Resistance" enacted by Elizabeth Stock, the significant, common thread is the isolated condition of the protagonists. All of them are "orphaned" one way or the other. The patterns can be summarized as "Isolation as Resistance."

If sometimes isolation is an unavoidable step for "resistance," it is no wonder that some characters choose to isolate themselves. As we see in the choice made by Miranda in "Old Mortality," deliberate self-isolation as resistance can be unavoidable when a character wants to *seek* a *new* order. If a sought order is something that has not been tried previously, it is too natural that a character cannot possibly avoid challenging the old order and a previously established system, *departing* from the former order, and placing oneself *nowhere*, that is, isolating oneself, at least for a while. Linking the resolute determination of Miranda to seek a new order at the sacrifice of isolating herself and the metaphor of an isolated individual as an island by Louis Forsdale, there emerges the imagery of the vast sea as representing the imagery of the period of isolation between departure and the discovery of new meaning.[3] As was mentioned in Chapter 1, Forsdale rephrases John Donne's words to metaphorically describe a condition of isolation, saying that each person is isolated; and comparing an individual to an island, Emily Dickinson uses the metaphor of "an inland soul" embarking "out from land" for the first time "to sea," grasping the profundity and the meaning of departure rather than describing the fear of the loss of the sight of the land. Although one need not physically go into the sea and drown oneself as Edna does, oftentimes, the imagery of departure from the previous land is interpreted as causing joy, even exhilaration, as Dickinson describes it in the following poem and as Miranda enacts it in "Old Mortality."

> Exultation is the going
> Of an inland soul to sea -
> Past the Houses -
> Past the Headlands -
> Into deep Eternity -
>
> Bred as we, among the mountains,
> Can the sailor understand
> The divine intoxication
> Of the first league out from land?
> (184)

Notes

1. I owe the titling of this chapter to the titling by Joan Schulz of her article, "Orphaning as Resistance."

2. As is quoted in the following note, Schulz emphasizes the utmost significance for female characters to express their voices through writing among all other acts. Although she titled her article "Orphaning as Resistance," the theme of "Writing as Resistance" is definitely a central assertion in her analysis of contemporary women writers and their female characters. Schulz's analysis is that female characters enact the process of self-orphaning through "constructing the self as a speaking subject" and that "[d]iscourse materializes possibility" (Schulz 105).

3. Schulz summarizes in "Orphaning as Resistance" that the forms of "orphaning" of the female characters of the novels she analyzes can be subsumed under the categories of "separation and reinvention." Under "separation" she includes such acts as "inattentiveness, refusal, and departure." Under "reinvention" she includes "intellectual and spiritual reconstitution, experimenting with new forms and directions for their lives, risk taking, future-orientation" and, "finding their voices," and says that "finding their voices" is "finally the most important step" for the female characters of the novels she analyzes (Schulz 104-05).

Bibliography

Bloom, Harold, ed. *Eudora Welty.* New York: Chelsea House Publishers, 1986.
————, ed. *Kate Chopin.* New York: Chelsea House Publishers, 1987.
————, ed. *Katherine Anne Porter.* New York: Chelsea House Publishers, 1986.
Booth, Alison. Introduction. In *Famous Last Words: Changes in Gender and Narrative Closure,* edited by Alison Booth, 1-32. Charlottesville: University Press of Virginia, 1993.
Brinkmeyer, Robert H., Jr. *Katherine Anne Porter's Artistic Development: Primitivism, Traditionalism, and Totalitarianism.* Baton Rouge: Louisiana State University Press, 1993.
Burgess, Cheryll. "From Metaphor to Manifestation: The Artist in Eudora Welty's *A Curtain of Green.*" In *Eudora Welty: Eye of the Storyteller,* edited by Dawn Trouard, 133-41. Kent: Kent State University Press, 1989.
Conrad, David E. "Tenant Farmers." In *Encyclopedia of Southern Culture,* edited by Charles Reagan Wilson and William Ferris, 1412-14. Chapel Hill: University of North Carolina Press, 1989.
Cooper, David. *Death of the Family.* New York: Panthever, 1970.
Culley, Margaret. "Edna Pontellier: 'A Solitary Soul.'" In *The Awakening.* Margaret Culley, ed., 224-28. New York: W. W. Norton & Company, Inc. 1976.
Dickson, Rebecca J. *Ladies Out of Touch: Kate Chopin's Voiceless and Disembodied Women.* Diss. University of Colorado, 1993. Ann Arbor: UMI, 1993. 9423479.
Eliot, Lorraine Nye. *The Real Kate Chopin.* Pittsburgh: Dorrance Publishing Co., Inc. 2002.
Emmons, Winfred S., *Katherine Anne Porter: The Regional Stories.* Southwest Writers Series, No. 6. Austin: Steck-Vaughn, 1967.
Forsdale, Louis. *Perspectives on Communication.* New York: McGraw-Hill, Inc., 1981.
Franklin, R. W., ed. *The Poems of Emily Dickinson: Variorum Edition,* 3 volumes, 1890. Cambridge: Harvard University Press, 1998.
Givner, Joan. *Katherine Anne Porter: A Life: Revised Edition.* Athens: University of Georgia Press, 1991.
————, ed. *Katherine Anne Porter: Conversations.* Jackson: University Press of Mississippi, 1987.
Gretlund, Jan Nordby. *Eudora Welty's Aesthetics of Place.* Newark: University of Delaware Press, 1994.

Gupta, Rashmi. *Adolescent Hero in the Works of Katherine Anne Porter and J. D. Salinger.* New Delhi: Atlantic Publishers and Distributors, 2003.

Hadella, Charlotte Cook. *Women in Gardens in American Short Fiction.* Diss. University of New Mexico, 1989. Ann Arbor: UMI, 1989. 9008391.

Hatchett, Judie James. *Identity, Autonomy, and Community: Explorations of Failure in the Fiction of Katherine Anne Porter.* Diss. University of Louisville, 1986. Ann Arbor: UMI, 1986. 8621446.

Hendrick, Willene, and George Hendrick. *Katherine Anne Porter: Revised Edition.* Boston: Twayne, 1988.

Koloski, Bernard. *Kate Chopin: A Study of the Short Fiction.* New York: Twayne Publishers, 1996.

Leary, Lewis. "Introduction." In *Kate Chopin: The Awakening and Other Stories, by Kate Chopin,* iii-xviii. New York: Holt, Rinehart and Winston, 1970.

Liberman, M. M. "Symbolism, the Short Story, and 'Flowering Judas.'" In *Katherine Anne Porter,* edited by Harold Bloom, 53-59. New York: Chelsea House Publishers, 1986.

Marrs, Suzanne. *One Writer's Imagination: The Fiction of Eudora Welty.* Baton Rouge: Louisiana State University Press, 2002.

Martin, Wendy, ed. *New Essays on The Awakening.* New York: Cambridge University Press, 1988.

McAlpin BVM, Sara. "Family in Eudora Welty's Fiction." In *The Critical Response to Eudora Welty's Fiction,* edited by Laurie Champion, 299-311. Westport: Greenwood Press, 1994.

Mead, Margaret. *Culture and Commitment: A Study of the Generation Gap.* New York: Doubleday, 1970.

Mertz, Paul E. "Sharecropping and Tenancy." In *Encyclopedia of Southern Culture,* edited by Charles Reagan Wilson and William Ferris, 29-31. Chapel Hill: University of North Carolina Press, 1989.

Montgomery, Marion. *Eudora Welty and Walker Percy: The Concept of Home in Their Lives and Literature.* Jefferson, NC. McFarland & Company, Inc., 2004.

Papke, Mary E. *Verging on the Abyss: The Social Fiction of Kate Chopin and Edith Wharton.* Westport: Greenwood Press, 1990.

Peel, Ellen. "Semiotic Subversion in 'Désirée's Baby.'" In *Louisiana Women Writers: New Essays and a Comprehensive Bibliography,* edited by Dorothy H. Brown and Barbara C. Ewell, 56-73. Baton Rouge: Louisiana State University Press, 1992.

Pingatore, Diana R. *A Reader's Guide to the Short Stories of Eudora Welty.* New York: G. K. Hall & Co., 1996.

Porter, Katherine Anne. *Flowering Judas and Other Stories.* New York: Harcourt Brace and Company, 1930.

———. *The Leaning Tower and Other Stories.* New York: Harcourt Brace and Company, 1944.

———. *Pale Horse, Pale Rider.* New York: Harcourt Brace and Company, 1939.

Prenshaw, Peggy Whitman, ed. *Conversations with Eudora Welty.* Jackson: University Press of Mississippi, 1984.

Price, Reynolds. "The Onlooker, Smiling: An Early Reading of The Optimist's Daughter." In *Eudora Welty,* edited by Harold Bloom, 75-88. New York: Chelsea House Publishers, 1986.

Schmidt, Peter. *The Heart of the Story: Eudora Welty's Short Fiction.* Jackson: University Press of Mississippi, 1991.

Schulz, Joan. "Orphaning as Resistance." In *The Female Tradition in Southern Literature*, edited by Carol S. Manning, 89-109. Urbana: University of Illinois Press, 1993.

Seyersted, Per, ed. *The Complete Works of Kate Chopin*. Baton Rouge: Louisiana State University Press, 1969.

———. *Kate Chopin: A Critical Biography*. Baton Rouge: Louisiana State University Press, 1969.

Showalter, Elaine. "Tradition and the Female Talent: *The Awakening* as a Solitary Book." In *New Essays on The Awakening*, edited by Wendy Martin, 33-57. Cambridge: Cambridge University Press, 1988.

Simpson, Martin. "Chopin's 'A Shameful Affair.'" *Explicator* 45 No. 1 (Fall 1986): 59-60.

Skaggs, Peggy. *Kate Chopin*. Boston: Twayne Publishers, 1985.

Tanner, James T. F., *The Texas Legacy of Katherine Anne Porter*. Denton: University of North Texas Press, 1991.

Taylor, Jane Robbins. *The Rural Poor Whites in Selected Literature of Mississippi Writers: Eudora Welty, Ewart Autry, Lola Autry, and James Autry*. Diss. University of Mississippi, 1991. Ann Arbor: UMI, 1991. 9130807.

Thornton, Naoko Fuwa. *Eudora Welty-no Sekai* [*The World of Eudora Welty*.] Tokyo: Kobian-shobo, Inc., 1988.

———. *Strange Felicity: Eudora Welty's Subtexts on Fiction and Society*. Westport: Praeger Publishers, 2003.

Tolstoï, Lyof N. *Anna Karénina*. Trans. Nathan Haskell Dole. New York: Thomas Y. Crowell Company Publishers, 1899.

Unrue, Darlene Harbour. *Truth and Vision in Katherine Anne Porter's Fiction*. Athens: University of Georgia Press, 1985.

Vanashree. *Feminine Consciousness in Katherine Anne Porter's Fiction*. New Delhi: Associated Publishing House, 1991.

Vande Kieft, Ruth M. "The Mysteries of Eudora Welty." In *Eudora Welty*, edited by Harold Bloom, 45-69. New York: Chelsea House Publishers, 1986.

Walker, Nancy A. "Her Own Story: The Woman of Letters in Kate Chopin's Short Fiction." In *Critical Essays on Kate Chopin*, edited by Alice Hall Petry, 218-26. New York: G. K. Hall & Co., 1996.

Welty, Eudora. *A Curtain of Green and Other Stories*. New York: Harcourt, Brace and Company, 1941.

———. *The Eye of the Story: Selected Essays and Reviews*. 1909. New York: Vintage International, 1990.

———. "How I Write." *Virginia Quarterly Review* 31 (Winter 1955): 240-51.

———. *The Wide Net and Other Stories*. New York: Harcourt, Brace and Company, 1943.

Westling, Louise. *Eudora Welty*. Houndmills: MacMillan Education Ltd., 1989.

Wiesenfarth, Joseph. "Negatives of Hope: A Reading of Katherine Anne Porter." In *American Fiction 1914 to 1945*, edited by Harold Bloom, 127-36. New York: Chelsea House Publishers, 1987.

Wolff, Cynthia Griffin. "Kate Chopin and the Fiction of Limits: 'Désirée's Baby.'" *Southern Literary Journal* X (1978): 123-33.

Index